Garsda
History and Traditions

Garsdale

History and Traditions of a Junction Station on the Settle-Carlisle Railway

by W R Mitchell

With drawings by Peter Fox

CASTLEBERG
1999

Garsdale is an interesting spot with its bog and drainage to north, west and east all within a mile – truly the watershed of England.

Derek Cross (1976)

If you got railway work in those days, it was reckoned you had a guaranteed job for life.

Tommy Harper, referring to the early 1920s

When I wasn't working, my enjoyment was country life. I went out with a gun. If I went through the tunnel near Moorcock Cottages, I could bag a black grouse any time I had a fancy to get one.

Richard Fawcett, alias Rabbity Dick.

At Dent, the train was waiting to tempt me and whisk me to Hawes through the tunnels: but not for all the blandishments of the railway posters would I have missed the green track that climbs between white walls by Shaking Moss… So I went on, and up, and up and down, to Garsdale Head and Hawes Junction, where the same train (or its blood cousin) was lying in wait for me again, ready to rush me through Yoredale.

A J Brown (1931)

Contents

For RALPH AND BARBARA LAKE

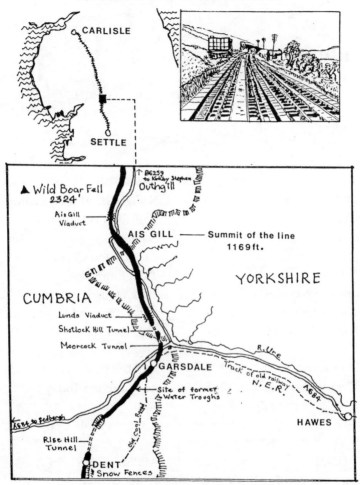

A **Castleberg** Book.

First published in the United Kingdom in 1999.

Text, © W R Mitchell 1999. Reprint 2001.

The moral right of the author has been asserted.

ISBN 1 871064 76 7

Typeset in Palatino, printed and bound in the United Kingdom by
Lamberts Print & Design, Station Road, Settle, North Yorkshire, BD24 9AA.

Published by Castleberg, 18 Yealand Avenue, Giggleswick, Settle,
North Yorkshire, BD24 0AY.

Foreword
by
Roger Hardingham
(a Committee Member, Friends of the Settle-Carlisle Line)

Garsdale from the Coal Road
Drawn by Barbara Lake

ON an April day when I visited Garsdale with thoughts of freight trains, sheep, lambs and daffodils, the gods of the weather had a convention. I stood near the signal box which, on its cliff-edge perch, seemed destined to be blown into the void. The southerly wind had much more of an edge to it than I had experienced in more tropical parts of the famous Settle-Carlisle. I held down my tripod and covered up the cine camera as the first flakes of snow appeared. Along the trackway of the Hawes branch, battling with the wind, was a solitary walker, cocooned in a blue anorak.

There are sunny days in Garsdale but more often I think of this frontier-station, between Yorkshire and Cumbria, for its climatic excesses, such as flurries of the famous Helm Wind from Edenvale and eager draughts which, funnelled by the fells, can meet you from two different directions at once. When the rosebay willow herb appears in bloom, you wonder if it began the process last year, or perhaps the year before that. Even the dandelions look careworn in a laggard spring.

I have known happy times at Garsdale, such as when dozens of photographers have been waiting for a steam special in the confident expectation that the sunny conditions will last. When I am there by myself, it is the sadness that manifests itself, and especially the sadness of the 1910 accident when a Scots express ploughed into two tank engines on Christmas Eve, with a fearful loss of life. Standing by the signal box, I think of the grief felt by Signalman Sutton when, having made a signalling error, he asked someone to tell Mr Bunce, the stationmaster, that "I've wrecked the Scotch express."

Overall, I think of Garsdale as a very special station. There is so much to think about, from the junction itself to the dances held in the tank house; from the Coal Road extending over barren fells to Dent to the little shop at the approaches to the station, which retained something of its Victorian flavour well into modern times.

It has been a delight to read the draft of this book and to know that so many memories will be put on permanent record.

Introduction

A sketch by Ernest Forbes

ERNEST FORBES, artist and newspaper cartoonist, visiting Hawes Junction in August, 1931, used the small ridge and furrow canopy of the main station building as an umbrella as rain slanted down. Then, reaching for his sketching pad and pencil, he drew his view of the isolated station and captioned the picture: "Two hours to go."

Hawes Junction was the original name for the station now called Garsdale. Then, as now, it is a meeting place of the winds, which often deliver rain and sometimes fill the air with snowflakes. Peering at the steaming drizzle on that August morning almost 70 years ago, Forbes passed the time drawing and chatting.

Two people shared his draughty quarters. On his Yorkshire tour, he had a friend. At Hawes Junction they met a local – "the man from Dent" – and were amused by his manner and dialect, which Forbes painstakingly wrote down. It was suggested to "the man from Dent" that "life in these hills must be very rough and rheumaticky." The reply as quoted by Forbes was: "'Appen. But they lives gettin' on to a 'undred aht 'ere. Me father's ovver eighty-five, an' e's getten all 'is faculties. There's nowt 'e don't remember!"

Forbes had been told that a Leeds train would leave Hawes Junction at 10.22 a.m. "And if we missed that, a guileless friend assured us, there were trains dashing through every two or three minutes. But on arrival at this place, and with two or three minutes to spare, we found that the 10.22 had always left at 10.15 and that since the 20th of July it had left at 10.5."

It seemed to the visitor that "most of the trains that dashed into Hawes Junction as quickly dashed out again – so quickly, indeed, that no live man could catch them." They must wait until 12.45 for a train that would "glide us gently into Leeds" by 3.30.

Forbes looked around. "Set down well below this very elevated railway was a row of desperate-looking houses, in which, I was told, lived the Stationmaster and his family, four signalmen, two porters, and divers platelayers and gangers – not gangsters." The three of them walked to the Moorcock. It was something to do. The "man from Dent" took his ale standing, remarking, now in good English: "When a man sits, he sits too long."

Thirty years after Forbes sketched Hawes Junction, capturing its bleakness, I made my first acquaintance with this astonishing railway station. I arrived by the Settle-Carlisle line and intended to travel to Aysgarth. The Wensleydale train stood in the bay, with a mixture of smoke and vapour curling from the little engine that would provide the motive power.

Unlike Forbes, I did not have long to wait. The Wensleydale train was waiting for me – the only passenger! I chatted with the footplate crew. The driver said: "Why doesn't ta hop up here. Thou'll be lonely by thissen?" I looked left, then right, and did so. At Hawes, the Stationmaster – complete with a cap that had "scrambled egg" on the neb – straightened his tie and peered intently into the carriages, little knowing that the only passenger was up-front, with the men who mattered.

Periodically, over the past 50 years, I have popped into Garsdale for a chat with the porter, for a cup of tea at the signal box or to record some notable event, such as the demolition of the Tank House. The space beneath the tank was once used as a social centre, complete with stage and piano. Was a Garsdalian pulling my leg when he said of a Tank House dance: "It was a reight good do – we hed t'piano ower three times?"

The station, a Victorian concept, now shorn of its many embellishments, sits uneasily on the landscape in an area of small farmsteads, field barns and walls made of native stone without so much as a dab of mortar to secure them. You'd think that over a spell of 130 years it would begin to feel at home. It still looks an imposition.

The Moorcock, much smarter than it used to be, boasts a sign that is more like a black grouse than the red grouse after which it was named. The species, sanctifed by sportsmen, is less common and widespread than it was before government subsidies for hill farming led to a wilful overstocking of many fells with sheep and the demise of heather, which is the grouse's staple diet.

Among the visiting sportsmen is Charles, Prince of Wales, visiting a friend at a quite large shooting box which is named Moorland Cottage. The Prince bestrode the platforms at Gardale but usually travels by car. He has visited the annual Moorcock Show. It is said that in 1991 when he visited Dent church with his landowning host, they conversed with an elderly lady who was one of the voluntary cleaners. Before they parted, she went home and returned with some free-range eggs for the Prince.

The road from Hawes runs through Appersett, crosses two bridges shaped like rainbows, then settles down to a relatively straight course but with impressive undulations. You might see a buzzard, circling high in the thin air. Gradually, the attractions of this dale-and-fell country are revealed. Just beyond the cattle-grid that is the entrance to Cotterdale, the present road – a turnpike – pretends to be the Big Dipper. The old route was up the ragged fellside on the right. The last time I went that way I came across some newly-hatched woodcock.

You will now see traces of the former Wensleydale Railway – a viaduct, a hump through which a tunnel was cut and then the grassed-over trackbed, beyond which, in due course, you will see the aforementioned Moorland Cottage. I have chatted with Pat Brown, son of Richard, the gamekeeper, who with his family occupied the eastern end of a building that has no less than eleven bedrooms.

Richard, better known as Dick, was head gamekeeper for C W (Kit) Garnett, stockbroker and landowner, whose grand home was at Chippenham, in Wiltshire. Each year, when the bonnie heather bloomed around Mossdale, he and his friends spent a fortnight or so at his Dales "cottage" and made daily sorties on to a moor that tickles the 1,500 ft contour.

At Moorland Cottage, a boiler set underground heated the place by sending hot air into the rooms through a large grille in the hall. The boiler was fed by coke delivered to Garsdale station, then transported to the house in a lorry driven by Jim Pratt or Mowdy Bill from Appersett.

During the 1939-45 war, Richard Brown attended to Garsdale Moor as well as his home patch. He carried on the traditional work of a Dales gamekeeper, destroying "varmin," burning rank old heather to encourage fresh growth – food for both grouse and sheep - and renovating shooting butts. His wife ensured that Moorland Cottage gleamed when Kit Garnett and his friends were expected for the shooting season, beginning on the Glorious Twelfth of August.

Local folk grew accustomed to seeing chauffeur-driven cars and a sudden influx of domestic staff, as each well-to-do visitor brought a supporting group, from butler to maid. As an influential landowner, Kit Garnett had the privilege of being able to stop an express at Garsdale station. Those friends who arrived by train were collected at the station by Mr Scarr, of Moorcock Farm. Parties of grouse-shooters formed a fortnightly rotation and most of the grouse they shot were consigned by rail to market in Manchester.

The high-lying district of the daleheads, through which the Settle-Carlisle made its way, was once rich in wildlife, and especially nesting wading birds. In spring, the melancholic whistle of the golden plover might be heard on the high moors, where the vegetation was thin. The whining pee-wee of the lapwing, known widely as tewit, announced that the season of awakening was at hand. A housewife at the Aisgill Cottages had to take care when hanging out the clothes on a line or she would have trodden on a lapwing's nest and eggs.

Curlews, lanky and streaky-brown, to match the landscape, came in on a sea-fret, which hinted at milder conditions. The ringing *courlee* of our largest wading bird was pitched above the toot of a passing train. Soon the dale-country heard the bird's bubbling trill as it glided over its nesting territory.

In summer, when the smell of new-mown hay drenched the air, young men from the railway cottages at the Moorcock and by t'Junction might find evening employment at the farms. A schoolboy, on holiday, became a sled-lad, riding a horse that drew a sled laden with hay from meadow to outbarn, where the hay would be tossed through the forking hole and trodden into a "mow" by more willing helpers.

Much of what I know about the World of Kit Garnett has come from Pat Brown, the son of Richard, who when he retired from gamekeepering moved to Grouse Hall, traditionally the home of the estate's underkeeper. Pat eventually took up a railway career. The Settle-Carlisle shouts to be noticed. Echoes are roused by the clatter of freight traffic. After storming the 22 miles of the Long Drag, where the ruling gradient is 1 in 100, a train bearing coal or gypsum rumbles across the Moorcock or Dandry Mire viaduct. The train vanishes from sight behind a row of Midland cottages that looks self-conscious in the Derby Gothic style of architecture.

The railway transformed Garsdale Head from a scattered community of farm folk into one in which most of the jobs were associated with the railway. The Midland line from Settle to Carlisle, built at great speed in the 1870s, impinged on the heads of several isolated dales, stimulating trade and giving what had been an old, settled local community an infusion of "off-comers."

A demarcation point in Garsdale was determined by the late, lamented branch line to Hawes and is still evident in an age when most people have the high mobility provided by the car. Folk at the eastern end of Garsdale, often referred to as Garsdale Head, look towards Hawes for their shopping and for medical attention. Families living westwards attend similar facilities at Sedbergh.

When compiling this book about Garsdale, my intention was to collect folk lore rather than to concentrate on the technical or historical aspects of the line. I was not disappointed. Some of the tales were fanciful. Adam Rudd, ganger, used to say that when a favourite dog got terribly old, he had it painlessly destroyed, then skinned it and made some leggings from the cured skin. When he wore the leggings, said Adam, a smile flickering across his face, he could run as fast as the dog had done.

A light-hearted story concerned the man who at a London railway terminus tried to book a ticket to Siberia. The booking clerk said: "I'll save you money by giving you a ticket to Garsdale in Yorkshire. It'll be a return ticket 'cos you'll want to come back!"

Pat Brown told me of the days when severe frost lifted the tracks until, as one permanent way man was fond of saying, with some exaggeration, "they went up and down like a big dipper." Pat and the other permanent way men were then on shift work, day and night, warning traffic of the conditions, which called for a sedate 20 miles an hour. The warning came from detonators placed on the track and from an orange light. At the time Pat spoke of, there might be hard frost for up to a fortnight at a time. Winter has been somewhat milder in recent years.

On our journey from Hawes to Garsdale station, we pass the Moorcock (if you insist!) and Moorcock Cottages, then drive under a lofty railway bridge. Into view, just inside the comparatively new county of Cumbria, comes Mount Zion, a Methodist chapel with typically steeply-pitched roof and a porch stuck on as though it were an afterthought. Incidentally, two-thirds of the Settle-Carlisle lie in Cumbria.

Garsdale station is set against a partly wooded fellside. A road that is a highway in a literal as well as a legal sense loses no time in gaining elevation to over 1,700 ft, crossing Shaking Moss on its way to the railway station at Dent. Until recent times, it was nobbut a green track known as t'Coal Road. The Midland Railway Company transformed Garsdale Head in the 1870s. What had been a remote farming community, served by dusty roads, became a junction, dealing with steam traffic on the Settle-Carlisle with a spur to Hawes and the line to Northallerton.

The Settle-Carlisle was planned as a fast, all-weather route to Scotland – a middle route between two keen competitors: the North Western and the North Eastern railways. Local traffic was not the primary consideration. The Midland Company must have its share of the lucrative Scottish trade. In 1876, despite a fickle labour force, monetary difficulties and appalling weather, the Midland had its all-weather route to Scotland and had put Garsdale Head on the railway map.

The sight of crack expresses thundering through Mallerstang, trailing sparks and smoke, soon lost its novelty for local people. The steam specials of today draw hundreds of enthusiasts to the lineside. Garsdale station is in an area of superlatives. Aisgill, a few miles down the road to Mallerstang, is the highest point (1,169 ft) of the Settle-Carlisle and, indeed, of any British railway. Hell Gill, a limestone gorge, nursery of the river Eden, has a name unrelated to the habitation of the Devil. The name hell is more likely to be derived from *hella*, a Norse word meaning a cave.

Garsdale Head, cut into true fell country, is ringed by an awesome assembly of fells of mountain status. It feels the back-draught of the Helm Wind, a cruel blast that plagues the western rim of the Pennines. It is maybe because of the wild and chilling environment that, in my experience, the fires in the Garsdale cottages are bigger and burn brighter than those to be seen elsewhere.

The small hill farms, once so typical of the Pennines, are no longer viable. Bell Pratt, who was reared at Round Ing, the farm at the head of Grisedale, though within sight of Garsdale station, recalls lives that

Railway Cottages

Garsdale Station
as it was in 1950

cock Viaduct.

Turntable

Wensleydale Line (to Hawes.)

Reservoir for Water Tank and Columns.

Island Platform with Awning.

Signal Box

Waiting Room

Platelayers Cabin

Water Cranes

Cattle Dock

Lamp Hut.

ex-Midland Rly. coach body.

revolved around the welfare of the stock – the gentle Shorthorn cattle and tough fell-going sheep. Round Ing had about 40 acres of inside land, or meadow. "We milked three cows, sometimes four cows, had a weekly churning to make butter, fed spare milk to the calves that were being reared and kept a few hens. We relied mainly on the income from 120 fell-going sheep. There was a living, not a fortune, to be made out of such a place."

Any surplus butter was taken to William Hodgson Harper's little shop near Garsdale station. The shopkeeper was there for over 50 years. He sold virtually everything, even feeding stuffs for cattle. Despite its remote situation, at the head of a secluded valley, the Pratts of Round Ing could actually see trains arriving and departing from Garsdale. "So at haytime you did not need a clock or a watch in your pocket. You could work out the time from the appearance of the regular trains. Your tummy would tell you when it was time for a meal."

In about September, local farmers would take horses and carts to Garsdale station for coal. Bell Pratt recalls: "You went to the station, helped yourself to what was in a wagon, then went down to the bottom of the hill where there was a weighbridge and you paid for what you had taken." Garsdale station was the place to visit if livestock or parcels were expected.

The cattle pens were well used. Some of Bell Pratt's relations were cattle dealers. Father's uncle, William Pratt, who lived at Clough View, was a dealer and also a Methodist local preacher. The Pratt family purchased cattle and sheep from Oban mart, where they were usually referred to by their initials – RB (Richard Bell Pratt), MS (Matthew Slinger Pratt) and JJ (John James Pratt).

They arranged for their purchases to be delivered to Garsdale by train. The Highland cattle, with their big curving horns, brought a Scottish flavour to the rich pastures of the Dales. As a lad, Bell Pratt keenly anticipated a train ride of six miles to Hawes. "This happened twice a year - on Whit Tuesday and on the day of Hawes Fair, which took place at the end of September."

My study of Garsdale, the only junction station on the Settle-Carlisle, is published just over 10 years after the famous line was saved from closure. The reprieve was announced by the Department of Transport on April 11, 1989. A year later, a memorial seat to Graham Nuttall was placed on the "up" platform at Garsdale and re-furbished in 1996.

Graham had been jointly responsible with David Burton in forming what became the Friends of the Settle-Carlisle line in the early 1880s. Graham was its founder-secretary. His dog, Ruswarp, became renowned as the animal contributing a paw-print to a massive petition against the closure of the line. They were both regular visitors to Garsdale until Graham's untimely death.

In 1999, the Friends planned a "10th anniversary express" for April 10, the train being hauled by a Class 47 loco in the livery of the English, Welsh & Scottish Railway Company. En route, it was hoped, the locomotive would be named "Ribblehead Viaduct."

It is proving to be a momentous year for the Settle-Carlisle, on which £1.6 million is being spent annually on maintenance alone. Railtrack announced it was investing £15 million in the system, installing continuously welded track along a considerable length of the 72-mile stretch. The new track will enable the line to cope with increased freight traffic and will accommodate heavier trains, as well as providing a more comfortable ride.

The Wensleydale Railway Association (WRA), formed in 1990, aims to restore services along the whole length of the route between Garsdale and Northallerton, creating the longest restored railway route in Britain. At an estimated cost of £1 million a mile, this has been a real leap of faith. On the stretch from Redmire to Garsdale (18 miles) there has been no track since 1965 and several bridges have been removed.

PART ONE

Garsdale Station

*Settle and Carlisle Railway has here
[Garsdale Head] penetrated a region through
which nothing but unlimited capital and
indomitable energy could have carried it.*

Rev W Thompson (1843-1895)

Though Garsdale station spreads itself along the fellside, it was never the huge complex that befitted the only junction station on the Settle-Carlisle. At the Junction was an engine shed but no goods shed; sixteen cottages for railway servants, attractively stepped to fit the local contours, but no detached Stationmaster's House, as in other places.

A viaduct to the north of the station was originally intended to be an embankment. The turntable, cruelly exposed to wind and weather, had to be provided with an airtight fence of upstanding railway sleepers. Even then, a goodly draught curled over the top. Garsdale was never short of water. Seventy inches of rain a year topped up the reservoirs that supplied water to the station and cottages and, further south, to the water-troughs, the highest in the world.

In its prime, Hawes Junction, as it was first known, had a Stationmaster's office, booking hall, porter's room, general waiting room, ladies' waiting room and toilets for gents and ladies. "The trains used to be packed wi' folk. You'd see a train arrive on t'down line. People got out and popped across the platform to catch a train going down Wensleydale. I've heard my mother say that if you wanted a seat on the Hawes train you couldn't get one. You had to ride in the guard's van."

Garsdale is distinctive. Its status as a junction led to it having an island platform at one side. On it were three stone buildings of modest size.

Elsewhere they would have been regarded as waiting shelters. If original plans had been carried out, the complex would have been on a grander scale. This was intended by the Midland to be a small passenger exchange station, with sidings for goods traffic and a "steam shed" large enough to accommodate 24 engines. No less than 30 cottages would be built to house the staff.

Two years later, a much smaller scheme was outlined, with plans for a shed sufficient for 12 engines and 20 cottages for workers. Even this was not fully realised. At first, at Garsdale, there were two signal boxes. The present impressively large box standing on the "down" platform supplanted these during the summer of 1910.

The station was first known as Hawes Junction but in 1900 became Hawes Junction and Garsdale. Thirty-two years later, the transition was complete and it became simply Garsdale. A minor concern of the Victorian stationmasters was receiving money from local farmers for the grass they mowed on the railway embankments. This became fodder for their stock.

In 1882, when Mr Foster was in charge of Hawes Junction station, he received monies from Robert Capstick, of Scar Top, William Thwaite of Mudbecks, Thomas Peacock of "Dandrewmire," and two Mossdale men, Adam Mason and William Sayer. The last-named paid him seven shillings for the grass on a one and a-quarter mile strip.

Garsdale was more than a railway station: it was the "pulse" of a small community in which Stationmasters, Signalmen and Porters were the heroes and their womenfolk the heroines. The age has passed when the porters at Garsdale had to clamber along the roofs of carriages to light gas jets.

Garsdale was closed in 1970 and re-opened in 1986 as an unmanned halt. Old-timers in the district are fond of recalling past servants, such as Harold Thwaite, who began his working life as a junior porter and stayed on until he was almost 70 years old. Also springing to mind are the Harper family, who kept the Post Office near Garsdale station. Edna Harper lived here for 82 years until 1995.

In 1999, the station is bring spruced up, though when I sat down with

Tom Algie of the Settle-Carlisle Railway Development Company to look at some old maps and photographs, we were conscious of many features that had been demolished. Gone from this "station in the clouds" are the tank house, the water troughs, the wooden awning round buildings on the island platform.

Long gone is the engine shed, re-built following a fire in 1917 which gutted a structure formed largely of railway sleepers. A lady who has childhood memories of the night when it blazed recalls the excitement as platelayers were being knocked up to help put out the fire. Happily it only held one locomotive – "one of those little tanker engines" - and there was none in residence at the time.

Gone are the cattle docks, the water-cranes, the VR postbox and the moving parts of the aforementioned turntable that was used regularly so that Midland locomotives on the Hawes branch might travel tender first. Once, battered by a gale, an engine was spun round, out of control, until someone had the idea of braking it by pouring material into the central well to slow it up.

The Settle-Carlisle is in good health, thank you. Sprinters – long and lean, like greyhounds – provide a seven-day-a-week passenger service. Sometimes there is the magic of steam traction. A "steam special" usually stops at Garsdale for water and on a humid day, observers see it as in a transformation scene at a pantomime. The air clouds with white vapour, through which the slow-moving, loud-beating engine suddenly appears.

Memories are sparse of the days when a man living down Garsdale cycled to Hawes Junction engine shed early in the morning to "steam t'loco up", so that the service on the Hawes branch would start promptly at 7 am. The station itself reverberated to the passage of passenger and freight traffic for 24 hours a day. The branch to Hawes was closed on March 16, 1959.

One man recalled for me the night during the 1939-45 war when two German bombs, possibly jettisoned by a plane returning after a raid on Barrow, fell in a field beside the Hawes road. The bombs went off with a considerable bang. My informant told me: "T'clatter wakkened me up!"

The best view of Garsdale station is from the Coal Road, which offers an unremitting climb to Shivering Moss on its way to Dentdale. The last time anyone went up the Coal Road with the idea of collecting some coal as fuel was in the General Strike, between the great wars, when no rail traffic was stirring but coal was needed for heating and cooking. The clear-weather views from the Coal Road are breath-taking.

To F S Williams, historian of the Midland Railway, and to many another writer on the upper dale-country, the landscape is "very wild and rugged". At centre-stage is Wild Boar Fell, one of the Pennine 2,000-footers, brooding over the deep trough of Mallerstang. Williams, in romantic mood, found its outline "grandly impressive" and noted that after sunset it "looms dark and terrible and seems to frown on all around."

A South Country man moved to the area and became a Lamp-man. He received a travelling allowance to cover the running costs of his car when on business. One winter day he mentioned to Pat Brown that he intended to cross from Garsdale over to Dent using the Coal Road, but Pat told him this route would be blocked with snow. The Lamp-man said he must try, but – said Pat – "it was not long afore he was back."

The Lamp-man now set off to Dent by way of Sedbergh, but at Lea Gate, with 600 ft yet to climb to the station, he could not find anywhere to park his car. The Lamp-man returned to Garsdale and walked over the Coal Road to Dent. It would have been handier for him to follow the track and go through the tunnel to Dent. That afternoon, when Pat was "leuking t'track," he again met the Lamp-man, who was returning to Garsdale, lamenting that he had missed some overtime and couldn't claim a car allowance for going to Dent. He hadn't got there.

Those who served the railway did so with enormous pride, even though the average wage for a platelayer in 1934 was £1.38, compared with the £1.39 of the Council men. Signalmen were on rather better pay. "The best-paid men were the engine drivers," said a woman who that year was married to a platelayer and could not afford to throw money about.

Stationmasters like Danny May and Cyril Breeze are well-remembered. Signalmen came and went at great speed, each seeking a better position elsewhere. At Garsdale, a signalmen had many a rough morning coping with several pick-ups, with trains from Northallerton – known as Geordies – and with main line traffic, both regular and special expresses on Saturdays and at holiday times.

Time and time again, I heard tales of indomitable characters. Adam Rudd, "a big-hearted fella and tall - six foot two," has already been mentioned. The temptation to return to him is irresistible. Adam built the black cabin that stands near where the cattle docks were sited. It was constructed with material provided by the railway and to serve the branch line. Such a cabin was well cared for, being regularly brushed with tar to proof it against the heavy Pennine rain showers. The big black iron kettle, which was found in every cabin, is now an antique, worth about £40.

Adam, who was at Aisgill before moving to Garsdale, could tell a good story. "He'd hev made a fortune today if he could have got on t'television." Adam told of a farmer "from across t'way" who one day approached him and asked him if he'd "sin owt of a big Swaledale tup on t'line." Adam, a keen gardener, later reported that the tup was in his garden. "It had eaten its way inside a turnip."

When he offered to look after some children while their parents were away for the day, he was told to "keep 'em away from t'fire." Adam later reported: "I built that fire up so much they daren't go near it. T'snecks on t'door were too hot to touch!"

Harold Thwaite, who was content to spend his entire working life as a porter at Garsdale was truly one of t'old school. An outstanding draughtsman, he was offered an office job at headquarters in Derby but refused it, adding: "I feel better 'ere. I know what I'm doing." Harold, a dalesman through and through, did not want a lot of fame and fortune.

This stiffly conscientious man wore a tie set against a stiff collar. Harold was tall, like Dick Thwaite, his dad. In 1951, when a relief Stationmaster dutifully plodded through the monthly accounts, Harold – who had been virtually peering over his shoulder while the work was done – said: "That's my job." After that, he was permitted to do all the work.

He was not averse to getting help but liked to check that the work was being done correctly. Harold was paid extra money for attending to the braziers that were lit at the Garsdale water columns in frosty weather. Harold would ask men who were attending to the points overnight to "pop" some coal on the braziers at two o' clock, then four o'clock, in the morning. Even so, Harold would be seen walking round at three o'clock, checking the fires to see they were big and bright enough. The water in the columns must not be allowed to freeze.

He asked a young platelayer who was walking towards the sidings if he would put two labels on specific vans. The lad agreed. Harold later went along to check that the labels had been correctly placed. Woe betide any railwayman who did anything without first acquainting him. Even when he was theoretically off-duty, Harold's restless eyes caught every detail of the working day. If, when Bonnyface, the afternoon train from Hawes to Bradford, arrived at Garsdale, some cattle wagons must be changed over, Harold would arrive to see that the duty man was doing it correctly.

To a child growing up in the 1930s, Garsdale station was special place. Here was a machine that dispensed chocolate, if a coin was inserted. It had the close company of cigarette machines. Garsdale was cut down in size in 1957 but as recently as 1971 much of the station was intact. The Tank House, a major accessory, constructed for the storage of 80,000 gallons of water, was demolished in that year. The 16 company houses that snuggle together as though for mutual comfort are now in private hands.

GRISEDALE CROSSING

To the north of the station, beyond the viaduct and tunnel, there is a traditional crossing point for Grisedale. Here are two stout railway cottages. The crossing point was boarded one day, and a metal footbridge caters for pedestrians, such as the many walkers who use the area. (A wooden footbridge was destroyed by fire one night. The blame was attached to sparks from a locomotive. Another story, widely believed, was that the bridge was getting rotten and somebody put a match to it).

Grisedale Crossing is part of a right of way leading from Grisedale to Lunds. In the days before motor transport became common, it was the shortest route for Grisedale farmers with their horses and carts who were heading for Hawes auction mart. Mrs Constance West, whose grandma and aunt were among the crossing keepers, wrote in the magazine of the Friends of the Settle-Carlisle Line that as two cottages were built there was always someone to open the gates. The first cottage had what were called the box-bells.

"It must have been hard work as the original gates were solid, painted white. Mr Samson Bowron, one of the painters, was quite a character who scattered marigold seeds around to brighten up the gardens. Once, when he was painting the crossing gates, he went into the house to have a drink of tea at break time. One of the nanny goats ate the paint which did not do the goat any good."

Children used the footbridge from the farms of Grisedale to and from school at Lunds. Bell Pratt, of Round Ing, was one of them. On the walk to their daily lessons, the children crossed the county boundary, from the West to the North Riding. He and his brothers and sisters would set off from Round Ing at 8 a.m. to undertake two miles of rough walking. They met up with scholars from other farms until there would be a chattering company of 15 or so. They were intent on arriving at school before the ringing of the bell heralded the first lessons of the day.

Of the crossing keepers, Mrs Jim Slinger was possibly the first. She was succeeded by her daughter, Mrs Betty Gamsby, who long continued the family tradition. Then, for over a quarter of a century, her daughter, Mrs Ethel Copeland, did the work. Before she could unlock and open the gates, to allow someone with stock or a vehicle to cross, she had to telephone Garsdale station for permission. It would not be given if trains were imminent, of course, and this could sometimes mean a wait of 15 to 20 minutes in the heady days of years ago, when 90 trains a day were operating.

The author first heard about the whistling ghost of Grisedale Crossing from Richard Fawcett, better known as Rabbity Dick, who began his railway career as a member of the local Slip and Drainage Gang. At mealtimes, or on stormy days, as the gang assembled in one of the lineside huts for a snack, fanciful tales were told. One of them, related by Joe Gamsby, was about the ghost.

Joe, a ganger, lived in one of the cottages near the Crossing, having married a daughter of Will Slinger, the first ganger to be appointed to the Lunds length. Dick's spine chilled on the day when Joe Gamsby told his strange tale. He was courting Bess Slinger and crossed the railway line to visit the family home. One evening, a shrill sound could be heard but no one inside the cottage commented on it. Will Slinger simply looked up from his newspaper and said: "It's nobbut t'Whistle."

It seems that when the railway was constructed, a ruined cottage had to be cleared away in the area where Grisedale Cottages now stand. A skeleton was found under the hearth of the old building. Fragments of red tunic and some metal buttons were also discovered and the remains indicated they had belonged to a Scottish soldier. The story that came down to Joe was that he had been courting a lass who lived at the old cottage.

One night, the father of the girl went out when he heard a whistle. The soldier was sitting on the garden wall, whistling for the girl. Enraged, the father struck down the soldier from behind, killing him. When the rest of the family went to bed, he buried the body in the ash-hole, a large square space under the hearth where ash from the fire fell, to be cleared out at irregular intervals. At least, that's what Joe Gamsby had heard and what he told his railway gang in the cabin.

Grannie Slinger told Rabbity Dick that one moonlit night, many years later, when a hard frost had crusted the lying snow, she and her husband went to bed, blew out the bedside candle, and heard t'whistle. Looking out of the window, they saw the spectral form of a soldier sitting within full view of their cottage. Whether or not he wore a kilt was not mentioned. Dick had asked Grannie if she felt scared at the sight. She replied: "No. Poor lad – he wouldn't harm anybody. He was just waiting for his girl friend to join him."

WIND AND WEATHER

The head of Garsdale is exposed to all the winds that blow – winds that might reach a velocity of 100 miles an hour. At such a time, so I have been assured, the signalman at the Garsdale box might feel his chair moving beneath him.

If there's any snow about, one of the first flakes will settle at Garsdale station. One day, when a "steam special" was due, I saw a white hillside turn black as dozens of photographers, hearing the cheerful toot of the approaching locomotive, threw off waterproofs, under which they had been sheltering from snow, exposing the bare earth. A local man remarked: "We've also got to put up with a lot of hill fog and drizzle…We're high up and get all the snow in winter. We've always survived."

J F Ferguson, an old-time Stationmaster, told me about the rampaging gales, and especially one that blew down part of a bridge. He and a companion, who set off to investigate, following the course of the railway, were unable to walk against the wind. "We had to link hands and use a route along the side of the embankment." The lofty heights and keen winds of Garsdale were a new experience for Douglas Cobb, a 29-year-old South Country man who became yet another of the indomitable Garsdale Stationmasters. He was promoted from the parcels department of St Pancras.

Severe blizzards were experienced in the 1880s and a Garsdale couple who "fed and slept" the enginemen working with the ploughs reported that work went on throughout the 24 hours and the beds she made up for the men were never cold.

Harry Speight, the Victorian topographer, in his book on Richmondshire, mentioned the "memorable snow-blocks on the line about Hawes Junction." As many as 700 men had been working simultaneously clearing the line for traffic. Speight recorded that on October 27, 1888, William Slinger, who lived at the Moorcock Cottages, was at work during a blinding snowstorm when he was knocked down by a train, being so badly injured he shortly died. "Singularly, his son was killed by a train nearly on the same spot about six years afterwards. Both father and son are buried in Lunds churchyard."

In the 1920s, the Midland, anxious to keep the line open after heavy falls of snow, stationed two ploughs at Carlisle and two at Hellifield. The Carlisle ploughs usually operated to the north of Hawes Junction and those from Hellifield to the south of the junction but the ploughs were available anywhere on the system.

The folk of Garsdale thus became familiar with the sight of a combination made up of two locomotives and their ploughs, set back to back,

with riding vans in between them, ensuring that the unit could work in either direction without the engines having to be turned. Each 26-ton plough, built on the framework of a discarded double-bogie tender, was attached to a freight engine, the plough being a straight scoop with a blunt-nosed front rising to its full height.

One van was used for workmen and their equipment. The other was for officials. Both vans were fitted with comfortable seats and a table. A coal stove was used for heating the van and to provide hot food and drinks. The van used by the officials had a fixed wash-basin fed by a roof tank.

In the coldest of winters, icicles, some of gigantic size, fringed the tunnel mouths. Mossdale, between Garsdale and Hawes, was especially dangerous to the footplate men because the locomotive went tender-first. The first train of the day had the unenviable job of breaking them. Any snowdrifts were cleared using brute force. "Sheets were stretched out to stop snow coming from above, but the stuff used to be squeezed between the floorboards and from t'sides like toothpaste out of a tube."

In February, 1931, snowdrifts closed the line for seven days, a locomotive was submerged and the only outward trace of the Mallerstang signal box was the stove pipe. "There hadn't been too much snow; it was the wind that did the damage." At about this time, the Settle-Carlisle was allocated new all-steel snow ploughs that fitted a buffer beam and replaced the large wooden combined ploughs and vans.

Journalists who visited Garsdale for the day infused some romance into extreme climatic conditions. Even DSB, writing in a railway newspaper, felt the Garsdale tingle-factor as he thought of preparations for the winter and for wintry weather. "As I boarded the local train that came panting up the hill from Hawes, and as we swept down through the fells – cold and grey now in the waning light – I felt selfishly glad that my lot was not cast in these high hills with their fitful sunshine, blasting winds and driving wintry snow.

"But when, in a few months' time, the snowflakes blur the window-panes of my office, turning to dirty slush in the busy street outside, and when I tap out on my typewriter the Press bulletin: The LMS Railway reports that snow-ploughs are working on the line between Hellifield and Carlisle, but it is not anticipated that normal traffic will be interfered with… I shall raise a metaphorical hat to the men who…keep the trains moving On Time – or, what is sometimes an even greater feat, keep them moving at all."

When the air filled with swirling snow flakes, the stoical folk of t'Junction were not particularly bothered. They had seen it all before and "put up wi' it." Polish troops, sent to help when the line was blocked in 1942, would not disembark from the train at Garsdale, complaining they had no wellingtons to wear.

In 1947, troops supplied from Hadrian's Camp at Carlisle had only mess tins and small entrenching shovels. The dixies were in grease, as for Norway. Men and food set off on the 10-35 a.m. train for Garsdale, but it might just as well have gone to Blackpool. The officer would not lead his men to where the snow lay deep and crisp. He said there was no native guide to show him the way.

That year, the folk at the station began to run short of basic food. A man walked to Hawes, a round trip of 12 miles, for some bread. A snow-plough was derailed by a build-up of ice at the Garsdale water-troughs. The plough was one of 20, assembled from various places, which operated here during the two months in February and March during which the line was closed to through traffic. At Garsdale, the contours were changed by drifted snow. One drift, between Ais Gill and Mallerstang, was up to 12 ft high and half-a-mile in length. Two engines were stuck at the Garsdale water-troughs for a fortnight.

Harold Thwaite, porter, recalled three years later: "Every morning in that 1947 storm I used to dig my way out of my house and then dig my way up the slope to the station. Things were a bit better there. Snow was lying on the rails up to platform level and packed down hard, so that I could walk across the track from the signalbox to the up platform like crossing a street.

"I spent the day digging and clearing and trying to keep the station clear, but it was pretty hopeless. In the cutting below the station, the drifts were thirty feet deep. Half a mile up the line, at the water troughs…two locomotives had been abandoned. The drivers found that they were running into heavier and heavier snow and they decided the only safe thing was to abandon the engines. They plunged out over waist-high in snow and fought their way back to the station through the blizzard. Later the locos were gradually covered until only their chimneys were showing. It was two weeks later before they could be dug out and moved."

During that grim time, Pat Brown, collecting mail from Edna Harper's shop beside the road leading to Garsdale Station, delivered letters to the seven farms of Grisedale. The daily walk began by crossing the fell to Blakemire farmhouse, which became widely known as the building which was "bombed" by the RAF. When the fodder situation on the Dales farms was critical, bales of hay were dropped from circling Dakota aircraft – and one bale went through the roof of Blakemire.

Wherever he looked, during that awful winter, there were dead sheep. "It was just like a battlefield." Some of the sheepfolds were stacked wall-high with the corpses of sheep overcome by the conditions. Not until the mild weather returned was it possible to bury them, a job carried out with the help of German prisoners-of-war. Pat never missed a round, though at times there was a white-out. Rations were transported to the families of Garsdale on the engine from Hawes. Fodder for the cattle arrived with the snow-ploughs.

Pat Brown has enduring memories of the 1963 winter. What happened? "Everything, really." He had been appointed sub-ganger at Garsdale. The ganger was in charge during the day and the sub-ganger at night. "We were cleaning points out in some terrific weather. In those days we did not even have a look-out man.

"If you were on the Garsdale cross-over, you looked out for the back-light on a signal – a small white light showing when the signal is set at danger. We could not always see it, but if anyone noticed it had gone off, we took precautions." Shortly afterwards, an express train would go rumbling by. That winter, days were spent digging out a locomotive and carriages which had been overblown by snow just south of Rise Hill tunnel.

Above: Garsdale at the turn of the century. Notice the awnings and the train on the branch platform. *Below:* Black 5 and "special". c1950.

Two views of Garsdale Head. *Above:* Looking towards the Junction. *Below:* Looking down the dale. The shop kept by the Harper family is on the left.

Hawes Junction in Midland days. *Above:* A distinctive sign. *Below:* The porched cottages.

Garsdale Station in 1950

A Hawes train stands by the branch platform. In the foreground is an ex-Midland coach body used as a store. Two goods trucks occupy the cattle dock.

The shop kept by the Harpers. *Above:* W H Harper, BEM, Postmaster and Carrier. *Below:* The shop. Notice the Tank House in the distance.

Garsdale Head.   No. 1932.

RAIN DISASTER
AISGILL MOOR-DEC. 24-1910.

HUTCHINSON. PHO

Disaster, 1910. The Midland express locomotive 4-4-0 lies on its side near burnt-out stock. *Below:* Garsdale Station in the 1920s.

Above: Hymn-singing in the waiting room, which was also used as a church. *Below:* Old carriage and Tank House, used for social events.

Above: Garsdale Troughs and Water Tank. *Below:* Black 5 (5407) with first
Cumberland Mountain Pullman, 1981.

PART TWO

Miners and Navvies

GARSDALE BEFORE THE RAILWAY

*M*ary was much pleased with Garsdale. It was a dear place to William and me. We noted well the public-house (Garsdale Hall) where we had baited...and afterwards the mountain which had been adorned by Jupiter in his glory when we were here before.

Dorothy Wordsworth was writing in the autumn of 1802. Her famous brother, William, having been married to Mary (nee Hutchinson) at Brompton, near Scarborough, the three of them were on a honeymoon walk across Yorkshire and into Westmorland, to a home at Grasmere.

They traversed Ryedale, crossed the Hambleton Hills and strode through the Vale of Mowbray into Wensleydale, calling at Hawes, the market town for the upper dale. They took this route because Wensleydale and neighbouring Garsdale extend east and west and are open-ended - a missing link in the Pennine chain of hills.

West of Hawes, the valley narrowed between austere fells. The trio were in Norse country. The grave, taciturn Norsefolk settled in small numbers at Appersett, Birkrigg, Mossdale and Lunds. William Wordsworth was achieving fame as a poet; he might also be considered for stardom as a walker. His long legs had carried him effortlessly across the Lake District. In Upper Wensleydale, he was in an area that would later be served by a parson whose name was Pinck and who clearly was in the pink of condition. Each Sunday, for almost 40 years, he walked a round trip of 11 miles in order to take the service at Lunds church.

The Wordsworths, crossing the watershed into the 10-mile-long glaciated valley of Garsdale, now picked up the River Clough, flowing swift and clear beside a scattering of 17th century stone farmsteads, many of them roofed by Baugh Fell flags. The trough-like valley lay between Baugh Fell and Rise Hill. The last-named separated the Garsdalians from the dwellers of Dentdale.

The chapel in Garsdale was a daughter-church of Dent without parochial privileges until 1562, when it won the right to hold baptisms and burial services. An old occupation road over Rise Hill to Cowgill in Dentdale – a route known to some as the corpse-road - began at Dandra Garth. In the opinon of the Rev W Thompson, this building might be regarded as the manor house. Mr Thompson's scholarly records about Garsdale were published in 1892, three years before his death. He referred to Dandra Garth as "an old-fashioned farmhouse with evident indications of former importance about it."

At this building, a curious coat-of-arms was cut upon a chimney piece. "This consists of a lion rampant, within a border of thistles, and is suggestive of a connection with Scotland, either in reference to the King himself or to one of his retainers. In the course of alterations, at different times, many human bones have been dug up on the premises, as if an ancient burial-ground had been there."

Thompson had been told of several farmhouses in the dale where similar discoveries of skulls and other bones have been made. "About ninety years ago, the then Duke of Cambridge is said to have visited Garsdale for the purpose of shooting on the moors and to have stayed at Dandra Garth. The clergyman happened to be both a crack shot and a good whist-player and the duke found in him a congenial spirit."

The Wordsworths, in their passage through Garsdale, would – if they chatted with one of the locals – detect local pride in the achievements of a local lad, John Dawson (1734-1820). He was born into a Quaker family and soon demonstrated that he was a mathematical genius. Instead of using this gift in the academic world, he worked as a surgeon at Sedbergh but meanwhile had among his pupils a number of first-class honours graduates from Cambridge. Each paid Dawson 5s a week for tuition.

Dawson's humble background is indicated by a contemporary

account. "His principal time for study was in winter, after the trials of the day were closed…He had no other light but that of a peat fire, situated on the floor – what are called by the country people heath-fires – the painful stooping posture necessary for availing himself of the light occasioned a violent bleeding of the nose, which, for more than a year prevented him from lying down in bed…"

The district through which the Settle-Carlisle was to be driven was, for centuries, traversed by pack horses, using a pattern of ancient tracks. The leading horse in a train wore a bell that alerted other travellers to its approach. Then came the turnpike trusts, who established and maintained routes on which tolls were charged.

One such route was that from Hawes through Mallerstang to Kirkby Stephen. At Collier Holme, about a mile beyond Appersett, the pre-turnpike road, used by coaches, followed the High Way, which made a rapid ascent to Cotter Clints. Here for about a mile traffic moved on a natural ledge of limestone, high above the valleys, to Hell Gill bridge, a structure that was old in 1675, when it was repaired at a cost of £3.10s.

The present road down Mallerstang was a product of the turnpike age. Work began in 1825 to provide a link between Kirkby Stephen and the turnpike linking Sedbergh with Kirkby Lonsdale. By October, 1829, it had been "properly made and was fit for the reception of travellers." It was then continued to Hawes and Gayle in Wensleydale.

The Galloway Gate, an ancient route much used by pack animals, followed the Coal Road from Garsdale Head to Dent, leaving Garsdale at Knows Foot Bridge, just below where the railway station would be built. From here, it ascended Garsdale Common to attain 1,760 ft at Cowgill Head. The name "Galloway" relates to a sturdy type of pony. The Gate was a branch of a famous old drove road to Scotland.

The rough track grandly known as the Coal Road served the pits of the Garsdale Colliery, which flourished from the 17th century until the 1870s when, of course, the Settle-Carlisle was open and deep-mined coal from South Yorkshire was available. Rough tracks led from the road to the shafts that were sunk to connect with the seams of hard, brittle coal found in the Yoredale Series of rocks. The coal sizzled and spat in local hearths or was used at the field lime-kilns.

A Coal Pit

Frederic Riley in his booklet *Dentdale and Garsdale*, "a handbook for the visitor and tourist," recorded one of the best accounts of working conditions at the pits. His information was based on chats with three natives of Garsdale who had worked at the pits in their youth. His informants, Thomas Edward Sanderson, Richard Handley and Matthew Haygarth, told him of gruelling conditions where the main shafts were at an elevation of 1,500 ft above sea level and in a bad winter snow was heaped against the boundary walls for 10 consecutive weeks.

Both horizontal and vertical shafts were driven into the hills. In the case of a shaft, the winding apparatus was a two-handled windlass, the men being lowered to a depth of up to 120 ft while seated on a clutch-iron (a metal bar). No pumps were available. The workings were always more or less wet. At times, a lively flow of water entered a shaft from below the surface, drenching the men before they arrived at the bottom. A proportion of a miner's wage of 14 shillings a week had to cover the cost of pit clothing, candles, blasting powder and working tools.

Low passages led to the workings. Through such a gallery, which often served as a water-conduit, the coal was "trailed" by a boy creeping on hands and knees. The boy was connected by chains attached by leather shoulder straps to a corf, which receptacle held about a hundredweight of coal. For this he was paid seven shillings a week, a sum from which a boy bought his own candles, leather knee-pads, trappings and chains with which to trail the corfs.

Frederic Riley heard from the Garsdale men that hours of work were so long that for several months in the year many of the miners did not see daylight, except on Sundays. And despite low wages and execrable working conditions there was no shortage of labour. Work of any description was welcomed in those straitened times.

In winter, during their walk to work from homes situated up to five miles from the pits, the miners carried lanterns. At the coalfield, high above Garsdale, the only protection from the weather for those on the surface were a few rudely-constructed wooden huts.

The coal was sold for five shillings a cart load. This consisted of 10 hundredweights, which was as much as a horse could haul over the moorland roads. Before the railway brought to the area the better coal from South Yorkshire, the stuff mined on the high Pennines was in keen demand. Sometimes, a score of carts – including the old tumbrel – might be seen awaiting supplies.

Curiously, during the railway building days of the 1870s, those who blasted out Rise Hill Tunnel, just south of Garsdale station, discovered a seam of coal. It was doubtless linked with those situated beside the Coal Road (known locally as t'Caw Raw). Well before the end of the

19th century, the workings were abandoned, having become water-logged. Many a shaft lies open to the sky. The area is not one that a visitor should explore.

Many years ago, William Stainton, of a farm bearing the curious name of Front, told Freda M Kay, of Sedbergh, about a drift mine on the fellside. He mentioned that the gritstone roof was supported by oaken props and that at no point in an extensive system was the gallery higher than four feet. Freda Kay, familiar with local dialect, was able to present the farmer's comments about Garsdale coal in his native speech: "Ah doubt it 'ud bi sheley stuff, but hot yance it gat agate. Ah've heard o' front bars bin burnt through wi' it."

The last person to take coal from this mine, early this century, was Lile Bobby Capstick. He lived at the farm for four years and never bought coal. "He browt up a couple o' lads, an' gey handy ther' were an' all – he used ta tak' 'em into t'drift, fill sacks wi' coal, and let t'lads crawl oot backwards, draggin' 'em." During the 1926 General Strike, a man from Dent opened up one or two of the old pits and local people collected bags of coal to keep the home fires burning. "If you've got nothing, it's surprising what you can do."

Long before the toot of a railway train was heard in Garsdale, it was a stronghold of Nonconformity. Methodist chapels proliferated. Bobby Capstick, farmer, took up local preaching, delivered his sermons without frills, in the homely tongue of the dale and, on his death, was buried in his native dale, the coffin also containing his hymn book and class-ticket.

In the 1860s, the thrustful Midland Railway Company, frustrated in its northern expansion by an unsatisfactory working arrangement with the London and North Western Railway, decided to drive its own line through to Scotland.

The 1860s were also a time of general emigration from rural areas into the burgeoning urban areas. The dalesfolk experienced agricultural depression and, simultaneously, an increase in rents. A major industrial slump occurred with the demise of lead mining. In many cases, families had derived their income from small-holding and employment at the mines.

Many families migrated from Garsdale and adjacent dales to Liverpool, which in its heady growth had become so isolated from the countryside by the Mersey and a Lancashire industrial conurbation that there was a grave shortage of fresh, clean milk. Enter the cow-keepers, who took the country to the town by having facilities for keeping cows, importing rich fodder to stimulate milk production, and delivering the milk to local customers.

The time came when almost every street in Liverpool had an attendant brick-built cowhouse, complete with hay loft, stable for a horse and a cart-shed. The complex was shielded from the outer world by high walls and wooden gates. Milk was taken from door to door and a dairy shop was open for business for 12 hours a day.

The diet of the cattle was augmented in summer by grass mown in the city's parks, cemeteries and road verges. The muck produced by the cattle was made available to arable farmers living close to the city. The city health committee ensured that each cowhouse was run hygenically. The family of W Metcalfe, who had farmed in Garsdale and moved to Fazakerley as farmer and cowkeeper, startled his customers in about 1910 when he began to use motorised transport.

The dalesfolk were accustomed to the grim working conditions – to the long hours of back-breaking work – and were sustained by the thought of addling [earning] enough brass [money] to be able to return to the dale-country and settle on farms there. A minority found better farms elsewhere in the north-west. The heyday of cowkeeping was pre-1914, after which came war (with the call-up to the Forces of able-bodied men) followed by a time of trade depression.

BUILDING A RAILWAY

The route of the Settle-Carlisle lay through an area where placenames hinted at the sodden nature of the terrain. They include Black Hill, Black Hill Moss, Blackmire and Dodderham Moss. The head of Garsdale became part of Contract No 2 (Dent Head to Kirkby Stephen), awarded to Messrs Benton and Woodiwiss, who also secured the contract for the branch line to Hawes.

Success in railway construction work was directly related to the number of men who could be hired. The contractors reckoned they would need to hire 1,400 men. They kept to this figure despite a high turnover of workers. Men were continually leaving for less arduous jobs or, in summer, to help with haytime. In 1872, it was estimated that a total of about 17,000 men had "jacked up."

A writer for *Wildman's Household Almanack* (1874) mentioned that in the "dreary" Garsdale stretch there was great difficulty in obtaining labour "although comfortable huts are provided and high wages given here." When, 30 years ago, I was asking local people for their railway memories, T H Harper mentioned chatting to Michael Wilkinson, who had died over 20 years previously – and he said the first locomotive to be brought up to Garsdale was on a wagon drawn by eight horses.

Miss Lilian Thwaite heard from her mother that when the railway was being made, gangs of navvies frequented the area and "it was hardly safe to go out at night." In fact, the criminal element was small. A wrongdoer was quickly hauled in front of the magistrates who were inclined to send him off to the nearest House of Correction.

The contractors made a start at Rise Hill, originally known as Black Moss. The area raised many problems, being remote from roads and villages. Here, too, "the side of the hill is breaking away in many places and the excavated matter is little else but what is called in railway parlance 'slurry' or slush. One of our informants remarked that it was nothing but slurry and boulders and that the slurry stuck to the tools like treacle." The slurry was removed by grafting tools and water buckets. Some of the water-marked boulders had an estimated weight of three tons.

Two shafts had been sunk from the top of Rise Hill to provide four more faces at which miners might work; they would also remain as ventilation shafts when the tunnel was completed. "At No.1 shaft," wrote a correspondent in the *Lancaster Guardian* (June, 1872) there are a blacksmith's shop, eight huts, miners' cabin, store-room and engine-house. The engine is a double cylinder one, of 25 horse power, and is used for blowing air into the tunnel and lifting the debris from the excavation."

At No 2 shaft were to be found a steam engine of 25 horse power and a double cylinder of 12 horse power for drawing up the steep ascent from Garsdale provisions and railway material. Also on site were a blacksmith's shop, a general store-house, a mortar mill, and five huts. "From the summit of Rise-hill we descended the steep incline at a quick rate in bogies. It was a trial of a man's nerves who was not accustomed to such a mode of locomotion."

The tramway was well used by the 350 men who lived in the hut-ments on the hill. At the bottom of the hill stood numerous huts, a weighing machine, stabling for 10 horses and a smithy. This "mountain tramway" – to quote Frederic Riley – was the scene of a tragic occur-rence in 1873 when the hauling rope broke, a number of out-of-control wagons ran downhill, and three men were killed.

The Rev W Thompson, an earlier writer about Garsdale, recorded that 11 people were descending when the rope gave way, "just as the waggons got to the steepest part of the incline and the trucks were preparing to rush down with fearful velocity. Presence of mind enabled one man to check the speed for a few seconds, by spragging one of the wheels, and nine succeeded in getting to safety; but two women, who still remained, were dashed to pieces and a man lying asleep across the rails was decapitated in a moment and never woke again."

Their "mangled remains" were interred in a single grave, in Garsdale churchyard, "and it was a memorable sight to behold the awed counte-nances of mankind – who had assembled to take part in the last sad rites."

F S Williams, when compiling his history of the Midland Railway, left us an account of what it was like to be in Rise Hill tunnel during its con-struction. The writer toiled up Cow Gill ravine and came to a small opening in the side of the hill – the temporary heading into the tunnel. "There is not much to be seen here, so we mount to the top, go as far as the first shaft, and taking our place in the iron 'skep', at a given signal are rapidly lowered in to the depths below."

The descent was "dizzying." Williams waited until his eyes were accustomed to the gloom. He and the others with him gratefully accepted the gift of candles. The party carefully picked its way to where the miners were at work, creating a subterranean passage 26 ft wide and 20 ft high. "After a long walk, we arrive at the face, where we see some 30 or 40 miners hard at work."

A man held a jumper (drill) that was driven into the rock by being struck by another man using a heavy hammer. Repeated blows drove the jumper well in and the hole was then packed with gunpowder and detonated to bring down more rock. In due course, dynamite – a relatively new explosive - was used, being conveyed to the contractors by road at a charge of £200 a ton. As Williams and his friends were leaving, they heard explosions. The ground shook beneath their feet. "The miners were firing the charges in the pit below." The rock was less firm than expected.

An embankment was proposed for Dandry Mire, near the Moorcock, but this area had an insatiable appetite for tipped material. Every tip wagon taken to the area had to be conveyed by road from Sedbergh at a cost of a guinea. A hundred wagons were in regular use. Tipping went on for two years but the continued wet weather and the loose nature of the bog merely caused the level of the mossland to settle 9 ft in a night and, at the edges, led to peat forming banks that were 12 ft or more in height. One bank extended 24 yards beyond the boundary that the Midland had negotiated with the landowners.

In 1872, frustrated engineers decided that the notion of having an embankment over Dandry Mire should be replaced by designs for a viaduct. It was to be built in the deepest part of the intended embankment. The piers and abutments would be carried down 50 ft through peat and soft material to the bedrock.

Messrs Benton and Woodiwiss had made some progress on the five and a-half mile long, single-line branch to Hawes. Readers of the *Lancaster Guardian* were informed that "the cutting at the junction is finished and for two miles from the terminus at Hawes the line is railed off...The road approach from Hawes to Moorcock and two occupation bridges and several culverts are finished and a girder bridge is nearly finished. A small-pox hospital has been built at Appersett for the men working in the North Riding district."

Emanuel Bramall, of the Junction Inn, Garsdale, regularly came before the magistrates for selling drink on Sundays or for keeping an unruly house. Drink made life tolerable for the miners in Rise Hill tunnel. By 1873 there were 120 men working here. The displaced material was being removed by way of two shafts.

The 1871 Census records eight boarders at Junction Inn. There were also boarders at the building opposite, known officially as Junction Loft and locally as Juggins. It occupied the point of land where the main Garsdale road met the older route leading from Grisedale. Soon after 1910, it was demolished, by which time Junction Inn had reverted to the status of cottage, being the home successively to Harold Thwaite and Tommy Harper and their families. On a windy night, if there was a strange sound outside, Tommy would remark: "It's only t'Juggins."

A visitor to the workings on Rise Hill noticed the "dimly burning candles, uncouth-looking wagons standing on the rails or moving to and fro." There were men at the facings, "some above and some below, with their numerous lights like twinkling drills beneath the terrible force of big hammers wielded by stalwart men." At each stroke, there was a "hac-hac or half-sepulchral groan." Also to be noticed were "the murky vapour, the chilling damp and the thick breathing."

The locomotive *Lorne* steamed between Dandry Mire and the northern entrance of Rise Hill Tunnel. By the end of the year, the permanent way had been laid over most of this distance. And still the work at Dandry Mire lagged behind, though by 1874 the piers and abutments were brought to the springing stage and four of the arches were almost complete. "There is no limit to working hours," wrote one visitor. The pay was a shilling an hour but the workmen tended to have roving habits, induced by bad weather.

By 1875, the Midland company faced pressure to get the line open for traffic. Costs were rising alarmingly. The chief problem in Rise Hill tunnel was loose rock. The continuing poor weather prevented a line being laid from Garsdale to the Moorcock. A delay of two weeks was record- ed at Birkett Tunnel, in Mallerstang, following a landslip. In October, 1875, the last stretch of line was doubled over the summit of Ais Gill from Mallerstang to Hawes Junction and iron ribbing had been fitted inside Rise Hill tunnel to help support the roof, two-thirds of which had been lined with bricks.

When, in 1875, the Settle-Carlisle was opened for goods traffic, Dandry Mire sank about four feet in 24 hours. Old sleepers were hur- riedly used to keep up the metals and to allow trains to pass over slow- ly. A small army of men raised a side-tip to give the necessary weight and stability, taking pressure from the bank.

Four months after goods trains were moving, readers of *Wildman's Household Almanack* were updated about the Settle-Carlisle. Aisgill, the highest point was reached from Hawes Junction via "a few dreary cut- tings." The Moorcock cottages, six in number, were for the men whose services would be needed to operate the new line. Masons were busy at Hawes Junction on the walls of the platforms and at some of the cot- tages. "The works, when completed, will form a small village...It is reported that a large reservoir will be made to supply the engines and other places with water."

A shed for a single engine was erected and not for long occupied by a Midland locomotive, being leased in 1881 by the North Eastern Railway. They provided the motive power for passenger trains operat- ing from Hawes Junction to Northallerton.

May Day, 1876, saw the inauguration of a regular passenger service on tracks that had been bedded down by goods traffic, which had begun running the previous year. It was reported: "The Settle-Carlisle stands quietly waiting for its first service passenger train. The lineside is bright with the spring grass – the contractors' regulation rye-grass and white clover, creeping slowly over the raw earthworks. Of the sta- tions, with their staff in readiness, Hawes Junction is not yet completed. In August, Colonel Yolland of the Board of Trade reported that, though lacking a clock, the station had just been opened."

There remained, for completion, Contract No 5 – the branch to Hawes. In September, 1876, the layout and details of a station at Hawes were agreed and over 300 men were reported to be working on the branch line. The major features were Moss Dale Head tunnel and viaducts over the gills at Moss Dale and Appersett. Progress on the branch was held up by heavy rain, also by the sudden collapse of an arch in Moss Dale Gill. Three men were injured. One of them subsequently died.

The Rev Bill Greetham, when he had spiritual supervision of St Mary's in Mallerstang, researched the part played by the church in ministering to those who built the local stretch of the railway. The Rev Robert Robinson, who was Vicar at that time, ministered to the families living in Aisgill huts, Birkett huts and Incline huts between 1870 and 1875.

Writing in the magazine of the Friends of the Settle-Carlisle Line, Bill Greetham reported: "I still have – and use – the Baptism and Burial registers that were being used then and have noted that 12 navvies, one wife and 11 children were buried in Mallerstang churchyard during those years." May Ridley, an infant from Aisgill huts, was buried on December 8, 1870, and 12 days later saw the burial of her father, William, aged 23. On May 28, 1872, two brothers, James and Richard Stephenson from Birkett huts, aged 21 and 23 days respectively, were buried in the churchyard, and on July 2 their mother, Hannah, followed them.

A memorial to those who died has been placed in the churchyard, which is within sight of the Settle-Carlisle where it runs on a ledge cut on the flanks of Wild Boar Fell.

Some of those who worked on the line settled in to the local community. Jack and Will Metcalfe, monumental masons, of Nappa Hall, Wensleydale, turned up at Garsdale during the construction period and their skills were applied to the building of the viaduct that was strung across Dandry Mire. Jack lived on the edge of the fell and then moved to various farms down Garsdale. He died at Garsdale Hall.

THE HAWES BRANCH

Appersett Viaduct

The six-mile-long, single-track branch railway from Hawes Junction to Hawes (where it would link up with the North Eastern Railway) was part of Contract No.5, awarded to Messrs Benton & Woodiwiss. Little work was done on the branch until the trunk system between Settle and Carlisle was operating.

Not until October 1, 1878, was Hawes connected with the parent railway and with the Wensleydale line, this providing a useful trans-Pennine route. The small engine shed was used by the North Eastern Railway, which usually worked the service to Hawes. As related, the engine shed burnt down in 1917. Rebuilt, it served the line until 1939.

During the construction period, the weary workmen were still having to work, as they had done on the Settle-Carlisle, in wind and wet. The principal works were Mossdale tunnel (245 yards); Mossdale Beck viaduct (four arches, 233 ft in length, 40 ft high); and Appersett Gill viaduct (five arches, 325 ft long, 56 ft high).

T'Hawes branch was a vital link with the east. None the less, this being dale-country, a homely system was possible. A footplate man working the Garsdale or Hawes pick-up might manage a brief spell of mushrooming in a lineside field between signal boxes. Men on a Hawes-bound train just before Christmas were known to have stopped near a berried holly tree and picked a few sprigs.

Houghton and Foster (1948) sensed the laid-back nature of the route: "Down the Hawes branch scream no mad expresses. The tempo of the Hawes track is unhurried. The trains move sedately. They are rather self-effacing and one feels that if anyone should be discommoded by one, the driver would be ready to stop his train, doff his cap with old-world courtesy and offer humble apologies on behalf of all railwaymen from Stephenson to Stamp...There are no passenger trains over the line on Sundays except, of course, in times of national emergency."

For years, no telephone link existed between Hawes Junction and Hawes itself. When a doctor was needed, two platelayers put their bogy on the line and rolled the six miles down-gradient to town. The bogy was retrieved by being put behind the brake van of the afternoon freight train. The platelayers held on to the draw-bar hook in turn. If there was a serious illness, the North Eastern engine was driven from its shed, sometimes in the middle of the night, and collected the doctor from Hawes, making a second trip to return him to his home.

Old folk have told me of a time when the locomotive was taken to the stockaded turntable at Hawes Junction because it travelled tender-first to Hawes. The fare was sixpence for an adult, half price for a child. Margaret Metcalfe has a special interest in the engine shed, if only for the fact that she was living near the station on the night in 1917 when the first shed, made of sleepers, burnt down. Margaret was only three years old at the time.

"I just remember seeing out of the bedroom window these huge flames. They built a new one, made of asbestos, and that stayed there till Beeching closed the railway down. Then it was pulled down. But it was there a long time."

Mrs Constance West, writing in the magazine of the Friends of the Settle-Carlisle Line, related that in the mid-1930s, when her father, a ganger, was given the choice of moving to Hawes or Blea Moor, his wife chose the former place. They found that no railway houses had been built except for the one to be used by the Stationmaster and there was no tight-knit railway community. "I always felt that I did not belong."

Adam, an old-time ganger on the Hawes branch, was "a big feller, who reared up into nothing; there's nearly a book to be written about him. He had a cabin at t'end o' t'platform at Hawes." Permanent way inspectors who slunk about the district, in case workmen were idling, included a man who was nicknamed Mickey Mouse. He was always creeping down ditches.

He was inclined to visit Adam's cabin unexpectedly, but Adam said he had mastered him. Adam had a gun with a bent barrel. It was designed to shoot round corners.

When Arthur, the son of Adam, left school he became a brickie, working on bridges and viaducts. The team of six or seven men was presided over by Taylor Dinsdale, who lived at Hawes.

Hawes Station

John Mason, of Hawes, was born four years after the railway came to town and worked at the local station from 1900-48. He started work at 15s a week and retired, as porter-signalman, at £5.2s a week. John, who worked at Hawes station at its busiest time, told me that one engine travelled the six miles to Hawes in six minutes. The passengers did not seem to mind being bumped about on seats that were not well sprung. The alternative form of transport was horse and wagonette.

He remembered when East Lancashire was thriving and thousands of flagstones and slates and building stones were being consigned from Wensleydale to the burgeoning textile towns. The quarries at Burtersett were rarely idle, stone being carted to Hawes on horse-drawn wagons. If there was an extra "push" at the quarries, carts were brought in as well.

All the surplus livestock went by rail. The lamb trade would start in August and there was a special train to Manchester on Monday evenings. Special trains were in demand in October, when the main sheep sales were held, and also at Christmas-time, when Hawes had a special fat stock sale, originally in the main street of the town and then at the new auction mart.

The railwaymen took pride in their engines. One man would use a certain engine for most of his time. He ensured it was kept clean and tidy. Mr Mason had known firemen who left the footplate as soon as Hawes was reached and busied themselves in polishing the brasswork and cleaning and oiling the motions.

Though the branch line closed in 1959, the track-bed is still clearly visible for miles and there are high hopes of restoring the system to enable trains to run, as once they did, from Garsdale through to Northallerton. If a ghostly train were to be seen on moonlit nights, it would surely be the ghost of Bonnyface, the Bradford-Hawes train, which returned to Garsdale at 4-25 pm.

The nickname is intriguing. Some people say the train was named after a particularly ugly permanent way inspector – one who "travelled half price; he's allus got his heeard and top part of his body sticking out of a carriage window." Another explanation was that as Bonnyface was returning about the time the permanent way men were knocking off for tea, its face – though begrimed with soot – was the bonniest they had seen during their shift.

After being idle for some years, Hawes station is thriving once again, as part of a Museum of Dales life. The buildings are being well used and an engine and carriages stand at the platforms. The big yard is now a car park.

PART THREE

The Census Records

Compiled by Paul A Kampen

HAWES JUNCTION 1871 TO 1891

With the building of the Settle-Carlisle line, the fells of the Western Pennines gained not just a railway line but also a new way of life for some of the inhabitants. Indeed, there was an influx of people from other parts of Britain whose accents must have sounded strange – even unintelligible – to the indigenous population. Looking at one part of the line only – that around Hawes Junction station (known to us today as Garsdale) – the census records are revealing and also pose some intriguing questions.

The Civil Parish of Garsdale lay in the District of the Sedbergh Superintendent Registrar. The Midland Railway built 16 cottages, instead of the 30 originally planned. These were intended for its employees at Hawes Junction station. This remote location lies at the extremity of the Eastern Garsdale section and the relevant census records are to be found in Kendal. The cottages at Moorcock, within sight of Hawes Junction, lay in a different county and their census records are today lodged at Northallerton.

Unusually, no separate Stationmaster's house was provided at Hawes Junction and that worthy lived in one of the cottages alongside his minions. The cottages themselves, like all the ones provided originally with the opening of the line, are part of the Settle-Carlisle scene. The line would not be the same without them. It is salutary to think therefore that in 1875 they were anachronistic to the area belonging, as they do, to the 19th century architecture of Derby.

In 1871, the work of census enumerator James Buck shows us that the railway had already swelled the population of Eastern Garsdale even though it was not yet open. There were 19 "railway huts" in three groups – Town Green (8 huts), Raygill (7 huts) and Shaft (4 huts). These huts housed many people. For example, Town Green Hut No.1 was occupied by William Cooper, a labourer from Leicestershire who was 43 years old. Also living there was his wife Alice, three children and six boarders.

Additionally, people concerned in the construction of the Settle-Carlisle were lodging at several farms including Skeltons, Ing Heads, High Scale and Low Scale. The family at Low Scale consisted of John Wilkinson (66), his wife Annis (68) and granddaughter, also called Annis (eight). They were clearly of a higher social standing than most of their neighbours as Mr Wilkinson is listed as a "landowner" rather than a farmer. Besides labourers, the lodgers included clerks, engine drivers and a civil engineer, one William Walmsley (30) from London. What did Mr Walmsley's Italian wife, Maddelena, think of a winter in North Yorkshire?

At Raygill huts, the boarder was Henry Cockett, of Kirkby Lonsdale, his trade being that of a "railway sawyer." This indicates just how many processes were involved in railway construction. Another sawyer, Thomas Barnes, from Orton in Westmorland, lodged at Raygill Farm with his wife May (22). They may have been recently married, for May was a Garsdale girl. Fellow lodgers were Thomas Masters, a railway miner from Devonshire (the exact place being noted as NK – not known) and Labon Gregory, a railway bookkeeper from Belper in Derbyshire. Their landlord, Edward Harper (50), farmed 40 acres; his wife was 37-year-old May and they had a daughter, Ellen, aged five.

The indigenous population was occupied largely in farming but there were other trades in evidence, for example a collier, a shoemaker and a nurse. A surprisingly large number of the railway workers are recorded as "Place of Birth NK." Sometimes a county will be given but often the letters NK on their own indicate that the person concerned has no idea where he was born.

Curiously, two farms were listed as "Mudbecks." At one lived

Thomas Metcalfe (26), who farmed 70 acres. He and his wife Agnes (43) were from Aysgarth. Mr and Mrs Metcalfe had a son, Ninian, aged five years. Also living with them were their nephew and niece, Edward and Isabella, aged 20 and 14 respectively. At the other "Mudbecks," which was of eight acres, the farmer was William Thwaite (54), originally from Wensleydale. Isabella, his wife, was 41 and a native of Garsdale. They had a daughter Betsy (11) and two sons, Richard, aged nine, and William, seven. (Richard eventually became a railway signalman at Hawes Junction station).

Thomas and Nancy Peacock, aged 71 and 57 occupied Dandramire (not the more usual Dandry Mire) respectively. Despite Mr Peacock's age, he was a working farmer in this era when retirement pensions were unknown. Dandragarth, a curious name originally signifying "Andrew's garden," was occupied by Betsy Cowper (60), who was the head of the household. To help her farm 65 acres were two sons, Edward (23) and Robert (20). Dandragarth had adjacent cottages.

In No.1 lived Ann Cowper, also a widow, with her son Christopher (9). No.2 Dandragarth Cottages, one of a group situated half way down the valley, was occupied by William Cowper (27), a railway labourer, with his wife Agnes (26). Their children, Margaret and Thomas, were twins, aged just one year. At No.3 lived Isabella Cowper (52), an unmarried nurse who lived alone. Clearly, this was an extended family, the members of which lived in close proximity to each other.

The Friends Meeting House and its attached cottage are listed as being uninhabited. Croftsthwaite House was another home where a railway family lodged. Miles Atkinson, the farmer, and his wife Sarah, were natives of Garsdale. At the cottage attached to this farm lived Jane Welch, the 20-year-old wife of a railway sub-contractor. With her was William, her two-year-old son and a month-old infant as yet unnamed. Mr Welch must have been working away from home on the night of the census. The Welches were presumably from London, where Mrs Welch was born, though young William had started life in Weston (Somerset). This family enjoyed superior status to their colleagues. They could afford to employ a servant girl, Jane Stainton, from Sedbergh.

At Scar Top was a large household. Richard Blades (48) was married to Margaret (56) and they had a daughter Jane (22) and son John (14). All four were listed as being born in Aysgarth. Mr and Mrs Blades's grandchildren, Edward and Richard Winn, aged six and 10 months respectively, were also in residence but were recorded as being born in Sedbergh. The circumstances may have been tragic as the two children were not just spending a night with their grandparents.

Ten years later, they were still living at Scar Top, with no record of their parents. Edward was by then a labourer and Richard a scholar. Was the fact that they were recorded in the 1881 census as being born in Garsdale a slip of the pen by the enumerator or a lapse of memory by Mr and Mrs Blades? Or could it have harked back to traumatic personal circumstances? Mrs Blades is now recorded as being a native of Cotterdale. Three railway-builders lodged at Scar Top. Charles Wright (62), from Dover, John Smith (19) from Towcastle in Northants, were labourers. John Williams (35) from Truro, was a miner, and living with him was his wife Eliza (3), who hailed from Bristol.

Many people joined the railway to escape from the drudgery of domestic service or the heavy toil of the farm labourer. The census contains an example of a man who left a skilled craft to become a "railway servant." He was John Dowbiggin (19), a native of Ingleton who resided at a cottage known as "Knudmanning," about half a mile from Hawes Junction station. He was apprenticed to Samuel Davies, a shoemaker. (Dowbiggin later became a signalman at Hawes Junction).

In 1881, the population of the area had mushroomed with the arrival of the Midland Railway's so-called servants. The Stationmaster was George Wooding (29), a native of Odell in Bedfordshire . He was married to May (25), who hailed from Sibley in Leicestershire. They lived at No.8 Hawes Junction Cottages. Next door to them, at No.9, was Joseph Franklin (22), another Bedfordshire man. Franklin, from Chellington, was a signalman, married to Elizabeth (21), a native of Sheffield. Presumably, Joseph met his wife in that city when he was based there before his move to Hawes Junction. The Franklins had a 10-month-old daughter, Edith, who was born at Garsdale. Someone added to the records a note that Joseph and Elizabeth also had a son. No name, age or place of birth is given. Had the son died?

Beside the Stationmaster and his family, the Cottages housed four signalmen, four railway labourers, four platelayers, one railway porter and two railway repairers, with two cottages unoccupied. All of these were heads of households except for one of the railway repairers (son of the head) and the railway porter. This was Thomas Kindleysides (16), a native of Knock in Cumberland. He was listed as a boarder, though his landlord – John (39), a platelayer born at Blencarn was also surnamed Kindleysides and also hailed from Cumberland. John's wife, Annas (35) was a native of Garsdale. However, their four daughters – Mary (13), Susannah (12), Sarah (9) and Jane (6), were all born at Milburn in Westmorland. Thomas was presumably a relative, perhaps a nephew, of John.

Reuben Alton, of No.13, was not a railway worker but a coal merchant and a devout Methodist, being a local preacher. Reuben, aged 56, was born at Aysgarth, his much younger wife, Eleanor (39) having been born in Tuddenham, Suffolk. The birthplace of their daughter, also Eleanor, aged seven months, was Mossdale. Clearly, they had just moved to Hawes Junction in 1881 and had started a family relatively late in life. It may have been a second marriage for both of them. Mr and Mrs Alton's cottage was to enter Settle-Carlisle lore as the Temperance Hotel. No doubt they took in lodgers who were strictly forbidden to touch alcohol.

Only three females residing permanently in the cottages were listed as having employment other than that of wife or scholar. Two of them, Mary and Margaret Handley, were the wife (60) and daughter (21) respectively of Richard Handley (58), a railway repairer who lived at No.6. Someone added the word "contractor" to the records so Mr Handley was possibly not a Midland Railway employee as such. Each of the ladies was a dressmaker and all three hailed from Garsdale, as did a granddaughter, Mary, aged four years. Was Miss Handley an unmarried mother or could Mary be the child of another offspring of Richard and Mary, snr? Living with the Handleys was John, a 24-year-old son, who also worked as a railway repairer. The surname Handley was very common in Garsdale at that time.

Jane Watson (18), a nurse from Liverpool, the third lady listed as having a profession of her own, was unmarried but had a daughter called Mary J Watson, born just over the hill in Grisedale three months previously. Jane and Mary J lived in the home of Christopher and Mary Thompson at No.12. He was a railway labourer from Crosby Garrett in Cumberland. The Thompsons, aged 30 and 19 respectively, had a three-year-old daughter named Esther and a two-week-old son called John, the latter's name being marked with a cross. Does this denote a tragedy in this age of high infant mortality? Jane Watson's relationship to the Thompsons was given as "servant." As a Victorian railway labourer was unlikely to have been able to afford domestic help, could it be that Jane was lodging in order to look after a sick baby?

Sarah Barton, another nurse, was at the time of the census visiting Charles and Mary Hopkins, who lived at No.7. Charles, a signalman, had moved around in the 27 years of his life up to 1881. He was born in Wesmancote, Worcestershire, and at some point met Mary, also 27 years old, who was born in Feltwell, Norfolk. Nurse Barton, a widow of 53, was a native of Munford, Norfolk, being presumably the sister or, more likely, the mother of Mary.

As to the older dwellings situated near Hawes Junction, William Thwaite was now a widower who was employing a housekeeper, Agnes Paul, a Scottish widow aged 53. Mr Thwaite's farm was now listed as Little Mudbecks, to distinguish it from the larger Mudbecks. The younger Thwaite son was no longer in residence but the elder, now 19 years old, was working on the railway as a platelayer.

Five members of the Bell family occupied Mudbecks. Head of the household was Thomas, who had moved from Wensleydale to farm the 125 acres. Jane, his wife, aged 32, was a native of Gayle and their children were Elizabeth (12), also born at Gayle, John (nine), a native of Sedbusk and William (six), born in West Burton.

John and Elizabeth Bowness, at Moorland View, were a married couple with two children Samuel (two years) and Dora J (six months). They farmed only eight acres, but Moorland View was also the Post Office, Mr Bowness was local grocer and provision merchant and he could afford to employ three domestic servants – Agnes and Henry Allen, 19 and 16 years respectively, plus young William Thwaites (16). At Dandragarth, Betsy Cowper was still in charge, with Edward to help her, but her family from the Cottages had moved on. Alice Rust, a widow who worked as a yarn-knitter, now occupied No.1 and No.2 was unoccupied, while in No.3 the sole inhabitant was Thomas Haggart (74), a widower whose work was that of sexton.

A man named Thomas Peacock, who headed the household at Dandramire, was clearly not the same Thomas Peacock who was there a decade before. The reigning Thomas was a widower with three young children – two sons, aged 11 and 7 and a daughter who was only two years old. He was, perhaps, the son of the previous Thomas. He employed, as domestic servant, Jane Thompson from Ravenstonedale.

Census returns demonstrate how, in the latter part of the 19th century, moving house had become an accepted part of life. The Industrial Revolution, with its greatly improved transport – in this case, the railway – had altered the pattern of life for those who are now referred to as the working classes and who in ancient time had travelled no farther than a reasonable walking distance.

Associated with the Cottages at Hawes Junction, through work on the Settle-Carlisle, were people from Lancashire and the southern part of the West Riding of Yorkshire; from Leicestershire, Bedfordshire, Worcestershire, Suffolk and Norfolk. Incomers from Milnthorpe, Milburn and Knock represented Westmorland and from Cumberland came a native of Blencarn, the small village in the shadow of the northern Pennines. Two Nottinghamshire origins were Cuckney and Skeby. Here, too, were folk from Durham and a scattering of places in the northern parts of the far-flung Yorkshire Ridings.

The 1891 census introduced several names with a hallowed place in Settle-Carlisle lore. The Stationmaster now was William Henry Bunce (39), who hailed from Hursley in Hampshire. His railway career might be mapped according to the places of birth of his family. Ellen, his wife, aged 36, was born in Holmsfield in Derbyshire. Her father, Samuel Bennett, a retired farm bailiff and widower, was aged 86. It is not clear from his residence at Hawes Junction if he was a visitor or was making his home with his kinsfolk.

It is perhaps indicative of the high social standing of a Stationmaster that the census enumerator had taken great care to record the Bunce daughters' middle names. Where there was not enough room, the initials are still included. The oldest of the Bunce daughters was Laura Helene (15), born at Dronfield and now a pupil-teacher at Lunds School. The others were Ellen Elizabeth (13, also of Dronfield) who had left school to become "mother's help," Althea G M (12) and Emily Agnes (nine), the last two having been born in Ashwell.

Next door to the Bunces lived a man who unwittingly and tragically became the most famous Settle-Carlisle railwayman of them all. He was Alfred Sutton, an account of whose career is given in the 1910 accident report. This indicates that he was newly promoted to Hawes Junction and, although married, was alone in the house on the night of the census. Three doors away lived John Simpson (to whom Sutton uttered those famous words – "go and tell Mr Bunce that I am afraid that I have wrecked the Scotch Express"). John Simpson, aged 32 and a native of Kirkby Stephen, lived with his wife Mary, a daughter – also named Mary – and son, George Stephenson Simpson. His wife was also 32 and hailed from Aysgarth. Presumably, he had been promoted from Hawes itself where his children had been born 10 and two years previously.

Two doors from the Simpson family lived John Blades, whom we met earlier. He was of the family who resided at Scar Top in 1871, being now head of his own large family and employed as a railway platelayer. John had married a Scottish lady, Violet Ann, aged 34. (The enumerator had not bothered to identify where in Scotland was Mrs Blades place of origin). They had five children – Richard (12), John (10) and Margaret (7), who were scholars, and their sisters, Jessie (four) and Betsy Jane (seven months) who were still too young to attend school. The Blades children had the company of their grandmother, Jessie Fothergill. Whether or not she was a visitor or lodger we do not know.

However, this Mrs Fothergill, a 67-year-old widow, was clearly a lady of substance. The enumerator recorded her as "living on her means."

At the Cottage between those occupied by the Blades and Simpson families the enumerator found Joseph Raw, a platelayer who had been born in Liverpool. His wife, Jane, was a local girl but their elder child (Margaret, aged three) had been born in her father's home city. A son, Henry Dawson Raw, had been born to Joseph and Jane Raw in Sedbergh, six months before, so perhaps Mr Raw had just moved to Garsdale. He later became ganger in charge of the Hawes branch and was heavily involved in the rescue work after the 1910 accident.

Another well-known Settle-Carlisle family were the Dilleys. In 1891 Henry, a 36-year-old native of Clifton in Bedfordshire headed the family. He was married to Jane. Mr Dilley was a signalman at Hawes Junction but when his eldest son, Walter, was born 16 years before, he still lived in Bedfordshire. Walter, now a porter at Hawes Junction, had two younger brothers – Roger, aged nine, born in Leagrove, and Ezra, whose life began five years previously at Stanford (Bedfordshire). Roger Dilley became a signalman and then Stationmaster at Ribblehead.

At the so-called Temperance Hotel, Mr and Mrs Alton had added another daughter to their household. She was Lydia, now aged seven. Mr Alton appears to have given up his preaching activities and to have added the trade of grocer to his work as coal merchant. However, few of the 1881 residents were still at Hawes Junction 10 years on. John Kindleysides was still in residence with Sarah and Jane, now 20 and 16 years old respectively. They were employed as general domestic servants. As Mr Kindleysides was still classed as married rather than as a widower, his wife must have been away from home on the night of the census and his two elder daughters had presumably "flown the nest." Christopher and MaryThompson were also still there and now had a second daughter (Mary, aged three) and a son, William (five). Their household included a visitor, Edith Hannah Chapman, a 16-year-old domestic servant from Dent.

Interlopers from the North Eastern joined the employees of the Midland Railway in 1891. William Sharp, the driver of the Hawes branch engine, was from Easingwold, while his wife, Rachel, hailed from Richmond. They were installed in their own cottage, as was Mr Sharp's colleague, William Gascoigne, born in Newcastle and still working at the age of 66; his wife Mary had been born 67 years previously in Blake-Law. Their lodger was a stoker, John Braithwaite from Bedale, and visiting them were Mary Jane Proud, a 37-year-old married lady from Darlington and three children who were presumably Mrs Proud's offspring – William (eight), Mary Rixby (six) and Dorothy Ellen (two). The two older Proud children had been born at Barton-on-Irwell, in Lancashire, and the youngest had started her life in Crewe.

Garsdale Head post office, where for many years up to 1995 Miss Edna Harper would reign supreme, was now in charge of Mr Thomas and Mrs Elizabeth Oldfield. Both had been born in Clapham 35 years previously and were recorded as a grocer/farmer and a grocer's assistant respectively. Mrs Oldfield was classed as having a "profession or occupation," which was not the case with most of the local married women. Another grocer's assistant was Mr Oldfield's 13-year-old cousin, William, who had moved to Hawes Junction from Leeds.

The household included a general domestic servant, namely Alice Jane Turner, a 20-year-old Clapham girl. Perhaps she had accompanied Mr and Mrs Oldfield when they moved from that place to the head of Garsdale.

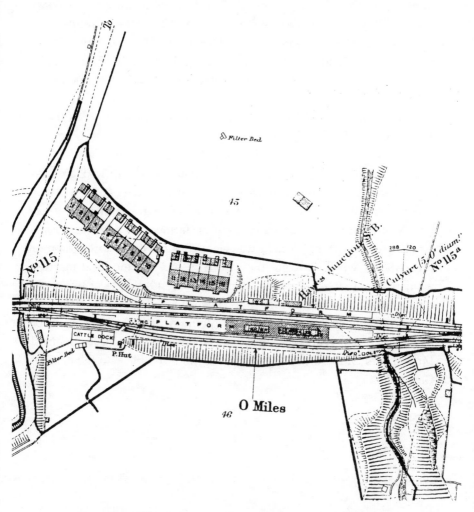

HAWES JUNCTION & GARSDALE STATION

PART FOUR

Station Staff and Facilities

Between trains, a chilling silence
descends on the countryside, so that
the thrumming of the wind in the wires
and the whispering of the sedge grass sound
ominous and eerie.
DSB (1937)

Garsdale station is set to look smarter than it has ever done, though most of the historic features – such as engine shed, tank house, turntable, etc – have gone. The smartness comes from a thorough restoration of what is left, including the lengthening of the platforms to meet modern requirements. With its branch line lopped off, Garsdale looked odd. The station was closed, then re-opened. Hopefully, in the case of Hawes, the branch will be restored through the initiative of the Wensleydale Railway Association.

Today, Garsdale is part of a regular service of Sprinters - long, grey and sleek, like greyhounds on wheels. "Steam specials" assuage their thirst under the admiring gaze of hundreds of train-spotters, who exult over a whiff of smoke and to the cheerful toot of a steam whistle. Diesel locomotives with rakes of coal wagons or containers marked "British Gypsum" commute through Garsdale on weekdays.

Garsdale is where the celebrated Long Drag from the Ribble Valley approaches the summit length of the Settle-Carlisle at Aisgill. There is an equally long drag from the Eden Valley. Generations of indomitable footplate men who thrashed steamers up from Kirkby Stephen gave a heartfelt sigh on seeing a distant signal nicknamed Star of Bethlehem, signifying the summit was nigh.

Steam traffic locally began with the fussy little contractor's engines. The dalesfolk would stare with drooping lower jaws as such engines were horse-drawn into the upper dales. Then, with the line completed, came the Midland locomotives. At first they represented an amalgam of ideas by two Loco Superintendents – by Matthew Kirtley and Samuel Johnson, his successor. It was one of Kirtley's engines (No.806), driven by John Mayblin of Carlisle, that inaugurated the regular passenger service on May 1, 1876. The Midland, with its new direct route to Scotland, gave passengers a ride in its new-style Pullman coaches.

The first Midland engines were painted green. The change to red, and subsequently to what became known as Derby red, took place in the 1880s, partly because the cost-conscious Midland discovered that red paint is more durable than green. Samuel Johnson had to double-head trains over the Settle-Carlisle until he could design larger engines with the 4-4-0 wheel arrangement. The 0-6-0 was retained for freight work.

Johnson built the first Compounds. His successor, R M Deeley, developed this class of locomotive, producing the 999 class. Ten of these superb locomotives were intended for use on the demanding Settle-Carlisle route. With their distinctive beat, the Compounds were the mainstay of the passenger services north of Leeds in the first half of the 20th century. Pride in them extended throughout the Midland staff. Harold Thwaite, the long-serving porter at Garsdale, and a keen amateur artist, painted a Midland Compound and for years this work was displayed in the porters' room at Garsdale.

William Stanier, a designer coaxed away from the GWR in 1932, became the Chief Locomotive Superintendent for the LMS. He created two standard classes – the 5XP Jubilee 4-6-0 and the Black Five 4-6-0. After teething troubles, the Jubilees became masters of the line, hauling passenger trains for the next three decades. In 1943, the first of the Royal Scots, rebuilt with taper boilers, were put in service on the Settle-Carlisle. For the rest of the Steam Age, these magnificent locomotives hauled all the express traffic over Aisgill and through Garsdale station. In the 1980s, Black Fives and Jubilees reappeared on the line hauling "steam specials." It fell to two ex-LMS Black Fives to haul the final

British Railways steam special over the Settle-Carlisle on August 11, 1968.

Most of the line's passenger workings were taken over by diesel locomotives in 1962-3, some five years before the end of working steam. For 10 years from 1968, steam was absent from the line but not from the memories of those who had driven and fired the trains through Rise Hill tunnel, picking up water at the troughs before rousing the echoes at Garsdale before reaching the summit of the line at Aisgill – and a blessed relaxation of effort on the long descent into Edenvale.

A man who became a fireman in the early 1950s had earlier been a "fire-dropper" at Durran Hill shed. He thought kindly of the "Midland line" because compared with engines on other systems comparatively little coal was being used. The fire had levelled off before it regained the shed, to the joy of those whose task it was to throw fires off and to attend to the bars.

The coal on tenders of locomotives operating from Leeds tended to be of better quality than the Scottish stuff, though "some of those lumps of coal were like tombstones. You had to set to with the pick and break them up. Or, if you didn't want to bother, tip the big pieces over the side." One summer's day, this man and his driver were travelling by Mallerstang when, as he put it, "this big lump of coal came down the chute. It was blocking the shovelling plate."

He pulled the "big lump" out and reminded the driver that there was a platelayer's cabin between Mallerstang and Aisgill. "When I saw yon cabin, I opened the footplate door. Pushed the lump of coal with my foot. Out it went. Bang. Split into two bits. One went down a bank and the other shot right through the cabin door. There were platelayers inside. I was scared stiff. I thought I'd hurt somebody." (The author's godfather, Ted Boak, had the same experience at Garsdale. He slowed down as a cabin approached. The fireman got rid of a large chunk of coal which demolished the cabin door).

The old-fashioned drivers knew the whims of the various types of engines and the foibles of the route. Carlisle men on the footplate of a train running south were aware of a lile bit of level track at Grizeburn.

"Then it was up again, through Kirkby Stephen and Birkett Tunnel. If you were really hard-up for a bit of steam when you got to Mallerstang, the driver would shut off and with a lile bit of level track and a bit more water in the boiler there'd be a bit more steam to play with. Then came your final slog to the summit."

A Carlisle man looking back on his first trips from Carlisle to Leeds recalls: "One old chap, Percy, a nice fellow, good mate, was driving one winter's night when I mentioned the lights in the old farmhouses scattered about the top end of Mallerstang. They were still burning if we were passing in the early hours of the morning. I said: "Folk must stop up late, Percy." He said that in the Midland railway days, following an accident in 1913 when an express ran into one that was standing, not far from Aisgill, the company gave some farmers a paraffin allowance so that they'd keep their lights on in case of a mishap on the railway. When that accident happened, everywhere was pitch black. They'd had a terrible time finding their way to get help."

When the new-fangled diesels came in, it was pie-in-the-sky to the younger railwaymen. "On a diesel you were not shovelling coal. You sat on your behind for mile after mile. If you'd fired a train to London, you'd shift six or seven tons of the stuff. This fireman, examined so that he might become a 'passed driver', was taken down to Hellifield on a goods train and brought back on the 'local', stopping at all the stations, to see how he performed. "It's easier now. It used to be said that some of the diesel drivers put an orange on the cab floor. If it rolled forward, they put more power on. If it rolled backward, they took some off…"

At Garsdale, in the 1930s, when it was a junction and the loco shed was working, "we'd put a few loads of coal off there for the engines." There was also a yard from which coal was distributed to local homes. "Hawes was a busy little station. The pick-up would come out of the town with 10 or 12 wagons and perhaps some horse-boxes. There were cattle wagons galore." The milk train operated six days a week from Appleby to Hawes and back. On Sundays, a light engine, obtained from a shunted freight train, ran from Garsdale to Hawes, collected the milk and transported it to Garsdale. The train then connected with the shunted freight and went to Appleby, where the milk wagons were detached.

To hear an old-time driver tell of life on the line was to come close to experiencing the true spirit of those who manned the steam trains. They might seem gruff but were basically kind-hearted. They had their own brand of humour. A Skipton man who was driving a No.3 goods engine, heading south from Carlisle on a hot day early in the 1939-45 war, stopped at Garsdale and picked up a man with a plausible story who then went to collect a most suspicious parcel. The driver told me: "We were not doing bad for steam but were overloaded. We all were at that time. We had to stop for water at Appleby and Kirkby Stephen.

"I said to my fireman: 'We'll stop at Garsdale. T'passenger train (Bonnyface) will have gone. My bottle's empty.' He said: 'Is it all right to stop?' I said: 'Oh, aye. T'passenger [train] will have gone and it's got to clear Dent Head before they'll let us clear Garsdale. Take your time.' We stopped at the island platform. While we were filling our bottles and drinking, this fellow appeared with a brief case. He said: 'Fine day, chaps.' I said: 'Aye – and you're getting your share of it.' He said: 'I'm getting more than my share of it…where are you going?' 'What for?' 'Because the only chance I have of getting a ride to Skipton is to persuade you to take me.'

"I asked to see his ticket. He had a day's excursion ticket. Settle to Hawes return. I asked him how he'd come to miss his train. 'Well,' he said, 'I thought I had time to walk it from Hawes to Garsdale.' He had allowed himself an hour and three-quarters. I said: 'Well, to start wi', it worn't enough time. And secondly, tha's bin calling at public houses.' He said he'd had one or two calls.

"I said: 'Oh, well – can ta keep thi gob shut?' He asked me what I meant. I said: 'Exactly what I said. If tha starts blowing it in a club or pub or anywhere where there's somebody 'at matters, about having a ride on an engine from Garsdale, two fellows on this footplate 'll get t'sack.' He said he could keep it dark. So he got on t'engine. He shoved his brief case in. He then shoved our lodging baskets to each side, then went back where he'd come from and returned wi' a roll o' sacking. In it wor a side o' bacon.

"We set off. There was t'Horton pick-up in front of us. It stopped at Stainforth and Settle. Then it was a toss up if t'Bentham pick-up had gone or not. We had Hawes pick-up behind us…As we entered the hole [Rise Hill tunnel], smoke were pouring out. It were one o' them days. Me and my fireman had our eyes on 'im. My mate said afterwards: 'His eyes came out like chapil hat-pegs when we hit t'smoke-bank and went in. I thought he was going to jump off.' When we got out, t'other end, he were the colour of a corpse. Blea Moor were worse. And, of course, it were a bit longer. He was standing at side where watter splattered in.

"He said: 'How will I get off at Settle?' I said: 'There ain't no difficulty about that. I'll stop. We'll put the water-bag in [use the water-crane]. When t'road is clear, I'll set you down on t'muck. I'll see you are on the road. Then you'll have to find your own way. But keep your gob shut.' I nivver heard owt from that day to this. Whether he told somebody or whether he didn't, I can imagine him swanking about a train ride from Garsd'l."

STATIONMASTERS

Those who were appointed Stationmaster at Garsdale did not stay long; they were usually cut-out for better jobs elsewhere on the railway system. An exception was Harold Thwaite, who resisted promotion and remained a porter at Garsdale for all his long working life. He knew the duties of Stationmaster as well as his own.

In 1910 and 1913, when two horrendous accidents occurred just to the north of Garsdale, the Stationmaster was Mr Bunce. Stationmasters recalled by Pat Brown were Messrs Banks, Simpson, Ferguson, May, Berwick, Cobb, Breeze and (the last to be appointed at Garsdale) Woods.

Douglas Cobb was described in 1952 as a 27-year-old ex-Royal Marines sergeant who stimulated an interest in station gardening and provided music on his accordion at events in the Tank House. His successor, Cyril Breeze, Stationmaster from 1953 until 1960, had a platform seat dedicated to his memory in December, 1998.

PERMANENT WAY

The work of the gangs who maintained the track was made tolerable because about every half mile was a cabin in which they might gather for meals or in especially inclement weather. It is only in recent times that permanent way gangs have been provided with waterproof clothing. Getting cold and wet was once part of the job.

The permanent way men were conscientious. Willie Slinger, when carrying out his Sunday morning examination, marked out such defects in a level that he saw. In the afternoon, he and his wife, with the lever pole, heel, shovel and beater, "tamped" the worst depressions. Willie tamped while his wife operated the lever.

The surnames Iveson and Metcalfe cropped up frequently in the workforce. Tom Iveson, who was a character and wit, applied for a sub-ganger's position. The Examiner came to a question about rail "creep" and tight joints. He said to Tom: "Tell me what you known about them." Tom allowed a few seconds for thought co-ordination and then he simplified what was really a complex problem by saying: "T'bugger's grows."

A man who worked in the "slip and drainage" gang, and who lodged at Garsdale in the summer of 1932, recalls that there was a ganger and eight men. You might be sent anywhere. The ganger had a pass on which was written: Carlisle, Leeds, Goole and Branches. The gang made a drain with a depth of 10ft "down t'auld Hawes branch, at a place we called Fred Cut." To reach Fred Cut, the gang travelled from Garsdale on a North Eastern train at 6-30 am and returned on Bonnyface, the only train the Midland ran to Hawes. The drain on which the men worked was intended to stop the bank slipping but this man thought "it slipped worse after they'd 'improved' it!"

It's surprising what turned up. Dick Fawcett, as a young ganger at Garsdale, heard of a loco driver who made an error of judgement which led to his engine toppling down the embankment near Dandry Mire viaduct. It was said that all efforts to recover the engine failed and it was eventually covered by ballast and rubbish. Dick mentioned in his book *Ganger, Guard and Signalman* (1981) that in the mid-1930s he had seen the chimney protruding from the embankment.

In recent times, Terry Sykes and Helen Smith re-read Dick's memories and secured British Rail's permission to visit the area of the missing loco. They took a metal-detector and on their third visit they got a strong signal from what turned out to be a chimney which (unhappily for their prospects of finding a complete locomotive) was lying upside down.

However, they did prod all round the chimney with a four foot steel rod and they had the loan of a Thorn EMI magnetic detector with a range of nine feet. Nothing large and metallic was found. So the old story of the "lost" locomotive must have been a spoof. Terry and Helen have written: "To the Victorian perpetrators of the joke, many, many thanks. It's been a fascinating project and, even in the mud and rain, very enjoyable." The loco chimney was exhibited in the waiting room at Appleby station.

The platelayers' cabin had a stove, with coal as fuel and a big iron kettle to boil some water for "mashing" tea. Most men had food in the handy sandwich form, corned beef being a favourite "filler." One man earned special comment because of his partiality for onion sandwiches.

Apple pasty and cake supplemented the sandwich fare. In one case, the "wee woman" was out of bed early to bake a pasty for her husband to consume that very day.

Few of the passengers who in heated coaches travelled through the high reaches of the Settle-Carlisle so much as noticed the workmen. Tommy Harper, ganger at Aisgill, did get some sympathy from a traveller. Tommy was helping to dig through snow on a bitterly cold day when an express stopped so that a pilot engine could be disconnected. A passenger, looking from a window, shouted: "My dad said that if you got on the railway, you'd have bread and butter for life. You haven't much jam on it."

Harry Cox, who worked on the permanent way before the 1914-18 war, was invariably away from home during the week, from Monday to Saturday. He sometimes stayed with an old ganger in one of the railway cottages at Garsdale. He was charged 2s.6d a week and the ganger's wife bit the half-crown he handed to her, to assure herself that it was real.

"The cottage had three bedrooms and there were six of us, two to a room. I often wondered where the ganger and his wife slept at night. Once we missed the last train from Hawes and had to walk back. We got into the house in the early hours. The old lady was just coming out of her dormitory. It was a cupboard under the stairs. The ganger also slept there."

Evenings were spent in light-hearted escapades. "We didn't do anything really wrong – the sort of thing that would get us into the bad books of the police. I do remember that when we were at Garsdale we walked into Dent to have a night out at the *Dragon* and the *Sun*. We returned home late, having had a gill or two. I remember that one of those pubs had a box on the bar. Inside was a smaller box, holding some snuff. You could help yourself to it."

A member of the "slip and drainage" gang lodged at Garsdale with a couple who had four children, "two lads and two lasses". The back bedroom was large and had an alcove. "If you wanted a bath, you went in t'river or you used a tin bath in t'wash-house at t'back. It was a grand big wash-house. To warm water up, you pinched a sleeper off t'side o' t'railway and cut it up for fuel."

SIGNALMEN

Margaret Metcalfe, as a child, was fond of visiting the signal box to watch the big shiny levers being operated and sometimes to have a cup of tea. Standing on the down platform, the box was handy to the station and to the cottages.

She remembers Dick Harper and Tom Oliver, who reared a large family at No.5 Cottage. "They didn't stay too long in the signal box. They seemed to come there, worked for a while and were then upgraded and moved on. A lot of the junior porters started there when they were sixteen. My brother, Frank Wilson, did. So did Fawcett Harper, whose father had the shop. And George Gamsby and Matt Fothergill...My brother had to go into the Army and then became a goods guard."

The Stationmaster at Garsdale had to visit the signal boxes regularly. That at Hawes was inspected daily and Aisgill came under his scrutiny once a week. He walked along a stretch of track that was open to every wind that blew. One of the unenviable jobs at Garsdale in the 1950s was for a porter to climb a signal to scrape ice off the red and green "specs." The scraper was made out of wood, adapted from minor pieces of packing used for the rails. "A man used to dip a rag in paraffin or methylated spirits and give the 'specs' a good rub. He had to be careful. A signal could go on or off while he was up there. It was a hair-raising job."

Many a signalman was partial to kippers. A van from Hawes toured the area with fresh fish and kippers for sale. Pat Brown, who remembered him from his youth in the 1930s, recalls that if kippers were required at Moorland Cottage a window was raised, then lowered on to a white towel, which was visible from the road. In the confines of a signalbox, which had not been designed for cooking, kippers were prepared by being laid on a toasting fork which had been home-made through twisting four strands of wire. As the signalman held them over the fire in a stove, there was a sizzling sound as fat fell into the flames. The ends of the kipper might curl and go black but the remaining flesh would be succulent and the smell was such that cats were twitching their nostrils at an appreciable distance.

Prior to 1914, almost all the trains using the Settle-Carlisle were double-headed. The long-suffering signalmen found themselves "cluttered up" with light engines, the drivers of which were anxious to return to their bases. An example of a man who suffered from a system that demanded too much from its workers was Alfred Sutton. At Hawes Junction he was involved in, though was not responsible for, an accident occurring in 1891. It was his signalling error that led to the notorious Christmas Eve accident in 1910. And this conscientious but hapless signalman played a minor part in the celebrated incident, when a gale was tormenting the district, of the locomotive that spun out of control on the turntable.

Sutton, as researched by Paul Kampen, was born in 1863 at Studley, Warwickshire. He became an employee of the Midland Railway Company in 1883 and two years later was a signalman. Moving to Hawes Junction in 1890, he was allocated a cottage next to that of the Stationmaster, William Henry Bunce, a Hampshire man who was 11 years older than Sutton.

With regard to the incident in 1891, this occurred on August 22 and involved an excursion train from Bradford to Aysgarth that was 45 minutes late because of delays at Skipton and Hellifield. Some of the passengers alighted at Hawes Junction. It was a time when two signal boxes controlled traffic. Carelessness by the Stationmaster and the engine crew led to the train being backed with force on to the buffers in the dead-end siding. The impact injured 18 of the train's 150 passengers. At the subsequent inquiry, the Inspecting Officer, Major Marindin, put the blame fairly and squarely on Stationmaster Bunce for not checking that the points were set correctly. Henry Hinsley, a guard, was also criticised. The Inspector accepted Sutton's testimony, for he did not believe that a man with a year's experience at a station would mistake the whereabouts of its water column.

So to the most notorious of the Settle-Carlisle accidents. The cause and effects were complex and have been fully elaborated elsewhere, but briefly Christmas Eve, 1910, was wild and wet. Sutton's spell on duty began at eight o' clock the previous evening. A tired man, he was still busy dealing with normal traffic, with relief trains and no less than five light engines, two of which, having piloted up trains early that day, waiting for the signal that would permit them to return to Carlisle.

Alfred Sutton, forgetting about those two light engines, Nos 448 and 548, pulled off the signals at 5-44 a.m., accepting into his section the down Scotch express, which was double-headed and travelling at 60 m.p.h. The drivers of the light engines responded to the signal, giving short blasts on their steam whistles. There is no reason to believe that Sutton heard them, for the wind was gusty and other light engines were sounding off as they moved about.

Sutton's mind had been on the express, which was now in the same section as the light engines. When those engines, trundling towards Carlisle at much less than half the speed of the express, came off the viaduct at Lunds, the double-headed express caught them up. Driver Richard Oldborn, on the leading engine of the express, saw a red tail lamp ahead and he applied the brakes. Driver George Bath, on the second of the light engines, glancing back, observed with alarm the headlamps of the express emerging from the tunnel. He saw sparks shooting from the chimney.

Driver Bath threw open the regulator and held open the steam whistle. It was too late to prevent an accident. In a cutting just north of Lunds viaduct, the express ploughed into the light engines, which were pushed for about 150 yards before they overturned at the mouth of Shotlock Hill tunnel. The express was overturned and the first two carriages telescoped. These carriages, being made largely of wood, and lit by gas from large containers, burst into flame as hot coals reached them. In the terrible blaze that followed the collision, six of the eight carriages were reduced to a heap of charred matchwood.

Blame for the accident fell on Alfred Sutton, though the inspecting office at the inquiry commended him for the forthright way in which he admitted his error. The crews of the light engines were blamed for not obeying rules. The Midland modified the signalling at Hawes Junction and began an extensive installation of track circuits on their main lines at junctions of any importance.

Jim Brown, ganger, was on his way to work that morning when, passing the signal box, he was addressed by Alfred Sutton, the signalman. This distraught man shouted out his poignant message: "Go and tell Mr Bunce, the Stationmaster, that I have just wrecked the Scotch express." Judging by a photograph taken at the time, grandfather was one of those who helped to disentangle the wreckage and clear the line.

Subsequently, Mr Hodgson Harper, the shop-keeper, general factotum and Postmaster, led a horse and cart loaded with coffins from the station, where they had been off-loaded from a train, to the scene of the disaster. A photograph taken by the *Daily Sketch* shows the cart was of the two-wheeled variety, with a white horse in the shafts. The horse is being led by Mr Harker. Walking behind the cart is a top-hatted, black-coated man, presumably the undertaker, who is using a large furled umbrella as a walking stick. Five children, standing in a line across part of the wide, unmetalled road, are the only spectators.

The interment of the 12 passengers who died took place at Hawes. Subsequently, and over a spell of many years, the platelayers at Garsdale, as part of their job, visited the burial ground twice a year to attend to the graves.

Adam Rudd, in conversation with Eric Bennett, for *John Bull*, in 1950, recalled the tragic occurrence of Christmas Eve, 1910. He claimed to have been first on the scene, soon after 5-30 am. "It was raining hard when I got there, but the fire in the front coaches was so fierce that the banks were blazing alongside the line. The express hit them so hard that the two engines were thrown off the track and pushed along like ploughshares...The front coaches of the express caught alight and they burned so fast that the passengers in them had no chance. I got there with my first-aid kit, but there was little I could do at the fire. I was told to help the drivers and firemen of the light engines who, by some miracle, were still alive. We put them in a hut by the line and started to pick out pieces of coal and gravel from their faces…

"When I went back to the train, I found that there was a little baby crying underneath one of the coaches. The child was completely hemmed in by wreckage, but as far as I could tell was unhurt. The weight of the coach was being held off her, but the space she was in was so small that I could not reach her, although I could touch her hands with a stick. I was just turning away to find some sort of a jack which would help me to get at her when a gas cylinder on the next coach exploded. My face was stung with red-hot ballast flung up from the line. When I could see again, the whole coach had shifted and the last wreckage of it was ablaze. The baby had vanished…"

Adam, when telling his sad tale, usually took away the bitterness by relating that he was wearing a new pair of shoes that morning. "Eighteen bob they cost me, and that was money in those days. Of course, they were ruined. And what do you think they gave for working all day at the accident? Five bob!"

As for Alfred Sutton, he moved to Leeds, where he was employed as a railway messenger – an experienced man doing a boy's job. His colleagues found him to be quiet and rather morose. He was doubtless brooding on events at Hawes Junction and, in particular, the day when – as he put it himself in a message sent to the Stationmaster – he "wrecked the Scotch express."

R A Kerr, writing to *The Dalesman* in 1945, felt to have a special association with the station. Because of a last minute decision by his mother, he was not a passenger in this express. "On another occasion, we had changed there. The train was drawing away from the station when it was discovered that my pram was still in the guard's van. Most obligingly, the Stationmaster had the train stopped and pushed back into the station so that the precious vehicle could be recovered."

Most of the time, signalmen were inconspicuous. They did their job conscientiously and without fuss.

Another grim accident, in September, 1913, was not caused by a signalling fault. Tommy Harper, of Garsdale Head, who told me about it, said that as a boy he went to see what remained of two trains and, many

years later, working on the permanent way as ganger, he found odd-
ments associated with the crash.

In this case, a sleeper train from Glasgow and Stranraer to St Pancras,
had halted a mile north of Ais Gill summit because the engine had run
short of steam, a consequence of poor quality coal. The driver of the
heavy train had requested a pilot engine but none was available. The
crew of a mail train from Inverness and Edinburgh, which was following, was also having difficulties because of poor coal. They were so pre-
occupied with trying to get sufficient steam they over-ran the signals at
Mallerstang and collided with the back of the stationary train. Fire
broke out and 14 passengers died.

The dead were interred at the cemetery on the east side of Kirkby
Stephen where, as at Hawes, platelayers used to attend to the grave
twice yearly. At Kirkby Stephen, the burial place is indicated by a long,
bench-like structure.

CATTLE DOCK

Garsdale handled cattle, sheep, even horses from Middleham, on
their way to race meetings. Margaret Metcalfe, reared in one of the cottages at Hawes Junction, recalls: "Often, during the night, I'd hear a
rumbling sound as Scotch cattle belonging to the Pratt family were driv-
en from the wagons into the dock to await collection. Sometimes, if they
arrived during the day, they would be driven down the Shop Hill, as we
called it, and as children we were terrified to death of their great big
horns."

R F Dilley mentioned when Willie Pratt, T T Iveson and Willie Moore,
senior and junior, visited Scotland, arranging for thousands of Scots
sheep to be transported back by special train. The sheep were unloaded
and let out on Garsdale Common. When these special trains were noti-
fied, the platelayers had to dig two or three graves as there were always
some sheep that were victims of overcrowding and must be buried. The
remains of dozens of sheep might be found on land above Garsdale

station.

Willie Pratt's first trip north of the Border took place to provide a change of scene when he was depressed following the death of his wife. He dealt with sheep as well as cattle. A man with a sense of adventure, he took the steamer to Barra, the Uists, Tiree and Skye. One springtime, he sent a load of hoggs (young sheep) via Garsdale to Redmire, advising his family by telegram.

Willie had three sons – Matthew, Bell and John James – the last-named living at Collier Holme. He made springtime visits to Oban to buy dairy cattle and would return with 40 or 50 beasts. Farmers who wished to buy some turned up at his farm and they haggled about the price. Bell Pratt lived at Clough View, not far from Garsdale station. He bought dark and stocky cattle from the Highlands and Islands. His brother Matthew had the more difficult task of selling them on his behalf, though they had filled out their frames through grazing the rich Dales pastures.

Bell Pratt was capable of many kindnesses known to few, or just to himself and to the person he had befriended. When he died, the usual notice appeared in the press, bidding creditors and debtors alike to make their claims and to meet their indebtedness. One farmer, who hastened to repay an emergency loan of money from Mr Pratt, was surprised to learn that his benefactor had left no written record of the transaction, nor had he mentioned it to his family.

James Pratt (1851-1927), of Chapel House Farm, Burtersett, grew up in an age when a Dales farmer, unsubsidised and doing his own bargaining when he had to buy or sell stock, was independent to an extent we can scarcely conceive today. He helped to change the farm life of the Dales profoundly when, with others, he founded auction marts at Hawes and Hellifield, which had good rail connections. Hawes mart was opened in 1885.

James had many contacts in Scotland, though he did not travel as often to the islands as did Willie Pratt and his descendants. James would go to Lanark and Stirling, to a fair at Kingussie, in Speyside, and – of course – to Oban, which had a speedy rail link, via Carlisle, with the station at Garsdale. He was frequently driven by horse and trap to catch the "Scotch express" at Garsdale. His daughter related that one frosty morning, when she had simply put a long warm coat over her night-dress, she was returning from Garsdale through Appersett when a local lady she knew waved her down, invited her into the house and gave her a hot drink.

She also mentioned that occasionally, when he missed a train for Scotland, Mr Bunce, the Stationmaster, would get him a lift on a pilot engine as far as Appleby. "If father had been only a few minutes late, they usually managed to hold up the train there." A few days after his visit, cattle began to arrive at Garsdale. "Sometimes, they'd shunt the cattle a bit roughly. Once we had a cow with a hip out. Father always had a law suit going on with the railway company for one thing or another."

When his daughter, Annie, accompanied him to the Caledonian Hotel in Lanark one autumn, the unusual bustle and preparations intrigued her. What great event was about to take place? The manager approached James Pratt and announced that it was in his honour. "You have stayed with us each year for 60 years," he said. James said to Annie: "It's nowt to get bothered about." Yet at heart he appreciated the gesture, especially as the directors of the hotel company came down from Glasgow and "we had a very nice meal."

In the spring, up to the 1914-18 war, James Pratt travelled by train and ferry to Ballymena, in northern Ireland, to buy horses, around 20 in number, mainly cobs he could sell to the Dales farmers just before hay-time. He sold the horses privately, so the "duds" remained on the farm. In the back-end of the year, he bought some sheep in Scotland. They were pure Scotlanders, as the Pratts called them. Up the slopes of Wether Fell they went. Annie told me: "We got overstocked with sheep in those days, and so they sent some for wintering to Brimham Rocks, above Nidderdale."

Local farmers collected their stock from the station or employed a drover such as Tommy Byker of Gayle to deliver them. The cattle usu-ally arrived on a late train and it was known for Tommy to walk them through the night. Of outgoing stock, the lamb trade began in August, when a special train left for Manchester on Monday evenings. Special trains for sheep were needed for stock purchased at the November sales.

Pat Brown remembers when cattle were unloaded for a dealer called Edwin Pratt. "They were Highland cattle. There might be two cattle wagons on a train of assorted goods. I have seen them fastened on the back of passenger trains." The wagons with livestock were put off into the sidings. A sheep show was held in land adjacent to The Moorcock in the "back-end" of the year. (The show now takes place in Mossdale).

TURNTABLE

Entertaining stories were told of the turntable. In 1900, a gale blew so furiously that a locomotive that had been put on the turntable was spun like a top for two hours until the movement was slowed by spilling material, mainly sand, into the centre well. That was the story – confirmed when I saw a telegraphic message, sent at the time, briefly reporting on the incident. (The former railwayman who had the telegram lent it out and it was not returned).

With the decline and eventual end of piloting, the turntable became obsolete and was removed several years before the end of steam haulage. The timber stockade that was erected to cheat the wind has gone. The table of the turntable survives in use on the Keighley and Worth Valley Railway at Keighley.

WATER TROUGHS

The Garsdale water troughs, just to the north of Rise Hill, had to be tended round the clock in times of keen frost. The 1,670 ft long troughs held between 5,000 and 6,000 gallons, about a third of which might be taken up by a tender in a few dramatic moments.

Derek Cross, who loved the Settle-Carlisle and recorded it through graphic photography, noted: "Why site water troughs over 1,000 ft up in the wilderness? Two reasons: plenty of water and, more significantly, it was the only piece of line that was straight enough and level enough for troughs between Settle and Carlisle. This fact, more than any other, to my mind, sums up just what a unique line this is: no gradient steeper than 1 in 100, but lots of that and curve after curve, all of graceful radius, considering the nature of the country."

The troughs were fed by water from a 43,000 gallon storage tank that received a supply by pipe from a reservoir on the hillside above. In that remote area, a small hut was built and a stove installed, to keep a man warm as he prevented the dam from freezing over. The water flowed into a tank at the lineside. A boiler was maintained to heat the water.

Some of the Garsdale men put in an hour or two overtime preparing a mixture which was drip-fed into the tank to keep the water clean and free-running. One element was to soften the water, another, known as "boiler tan," was to stop the inside of the boiler from rusting and there was anti-foam, to prevent frothing.

The troughs had cost the Midland £4,396, but when they were installed the big bogy tenders on the Compound locos could be jettisoned. Against the cost of the troughs had to be set £1,707, the expense of adapting the smaller tenders with the tackle necessary to pick up water. Harry Cox, who worked on the installation of the troughs early in 1907, told me that when the hillside reservoir was made, a stream was diverted. From 50 to 60 men were set to work making a concrete dam, materials for which were conveyed across the fell on a light railway.

"George Fawcett was the man in charge, with Bill Smith as the ganger. The work went on for nearly 12 months. During that time, the stream was diverted over the top along a chute. When the day came to use the dam, some 'top brass' turned up and the water was allowed back into its old course. The dam leaked like a sieve. Not enough cement had been used. Someone had been trying to save the Midland Railway money, which in the end was not the case. The work had to be done again."

To instal the troughs, rails were removed and the top soil dug out. Then slag from a steel works was laid in the trenches. "The slag was full of holes, like a sponge. We dug down for two or three feet...When the first locomotives used the troughs, folk gathered to watch 'em, as folks will. But the scoops were not working properly; they simply pushed the water out and sightseers were soaked to the skin." A device was added to the scoops so that it would "cut" into the water.

Collecting water at Garsdale involved split-second timing. "You had the scoop to wind down into the troughs. A concrete post with an oil lamp was supposed to be a marker at night. Being an oil lamp, the marker had usually gone out. So on a pitch-black night, you counted bridges. One. Two. At the third bridge, the scoop must go in. Sometimes, if you had to follow close behind another train, the troughs were still filling with water. Sometimes, if they were frozen, we had to make a water-stop at Appleby. And sometimes, if there was hardly any water left, the driver got a bit jittery in case we couldn't make Appleby in time."

Continued on page 97.

Steam Special at Garsdale

"Bahamas," a Jubilee locomotive, storms away from Garsdale in the early 1980s. The train, grandly titled Royal Scotsman, was a "special" from north of the Border undertaking a tour in England. Notice the upper quadrant signal.

Moorcock Cottages

Mount Zion Chapel

Winter, 1947. *Above:* A locomotive battles with a drift near Aisgill. *Below:* LMS 4F (44149), one of a duo working back-to-back with snow-ploughs, takes on water.

LMS Black 5 No. 5305 departs Garsdale on o

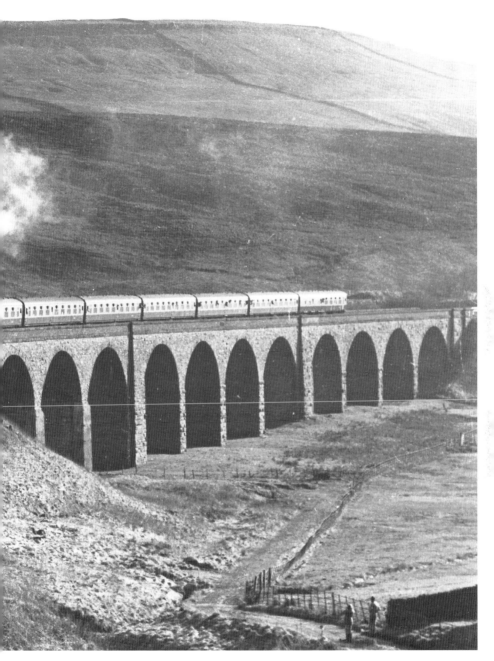

the first Cumbrian Mountain Expresses, 1980.

Above: The barricaded turntable at Garsdale. *Below:* Paul Holden at the frame of the turntable on the day it was removed to the Worth Valley line at Keighley.

Right: Washing day at t'Junction, in the early 1960s. The drying ground was known as The Green.

Left: Garsdale's celebrated water troughs as viewed from a BR 4-6-0 mixed traffic loco, in the 1960s.

Right: The signal box at Aisgill, which is now serving a preserved line in Derbyshire.

Farewell to Garsdale

Duke of Gloucester (BR 71000) having just crossed Dandry Mire Viaduct
for Carlisle, can relax a little. The exertions of the Long Drag are over.
Ahead lies a descent into the Eden Valley.

The art was not to put the scoop in too far and to take it out as quickly as possible or water flooded over, through a grate, and soaked anyone standing on the footplate. A fireman who did not care much for the driver would deliberately leave the scoop in longer than was necessary to give the driver a soaking. If the thirsty locomotive was hauling a passenger train in warm weather, it was more than likely that some passengers had their windows lowered and, as the scoop began to pick up water, spray rose and they got wet. It was the guard's duty to walk down the train and advise them to shut the windows. If there was a water shortage in summer, use of the troughs was restricted to express trains.

Big Bass was driving with a plough one day when the troughs were frozen solid. The snow had become packed on top of the ice. "Off he set, but instead of hitting and going into the snow, the plough rode up, the engines following. They finished up crossways, blocking both main lines and being about four feet from going down the bank…"

Steam-heating was introduced at the lineside to ensure a flow of water to the troughs. Dick Fawcett recalled that, in cold snaps, "steam-raisers came from the Hellifield Shed. The troughs needed attention when any spilled water froze hard. Ice, which also covered the track and sleepers, had to be broken up and removed by men using picks and shovels." A Garsdale man recalls: "We all wore clogs in those days. I could never really walk properly in clogs, let alone stand and work on the side of a sloping ice-field."

The workers slept in the platelayers' cabin and took provisions with them. Jimmy Antell and Bob Lund were on that unwelcome job for weeks. The crews of locomotives being thrashed up the Drag from Settle maintained that the troughs were unreliable. They froze in winter, dried out in summer and were blocked by fallen leaves in autumn. The only time they were available was springtime.

O S Nock, the railway writer, riding the old 40552, wrote: "With screaming whistle, she led us into Rise Tunnel; out again on to that dizzy ledge above Garsdale to the highest water troughs in England. The driver…lowered his scoop at 60 mph. The tender was evidently fuller than he thought, for in seconds it had overflowed and we, on the second engine, were smothered. Involuntarily, I ducked, for the water came over in a solid cascade and hit our cab glasses with a roar rather than a splash."

Pat Brown, who used to attend to the water-troughs, says: "In a cold snap, we'd hack the ice – two fellows with picks and one with a shovel following on behind. We had crampons on our feet; the spikes stopped us from skidding. The ice only came off in little bits, about an inch square. If a train came, and the weather really was freezing, you could hardly tell where you'd been when you looked back." The troughs were removed and sent for scrap in the 1950s.

PART FIVE

Social Life at the Junction

The feet-in-the-good-earth dalesfolk
took to their bosoms and cherished those
whose duty it was to work and maintain
the railway…The dalesfolk came to consider
it peculiarly their own.
Houghton and Foster (1948)

The long defunct *John Bull* of December 16, 1950, featured the "railway" village of Garsdale, under the heading "Change Here for the Back of Beyond." At that time, 90 trains a day passed through but according to the writer, Eric Bennett, the station was so isolated that the quickest way to reach it was by road.

This representative of a national magazine elaborated his thesis as follows: "Garsdale Junction is more than 1,100 ft up in the Pennines, just below the peak of that soaring system of viaducts, tunnels and cuttings which carries the Midland Region main railway line from Glasgow and Carlisle to Leeds, the East Midlands and London.

"It is a few miles south of the Westmorland border, a few yards west of the boundary that divides the West and North Ridings of Yorkshire, on the watershed which divides Wensleydale from Ribblesdale, and, although on the railway line, it is rather less accessible than the back of beyond. On weekdays, only half a dozen local trains each way stop at Garsdale Junction out of about ninety express freights and passengers, including the Thames-Clyde express, which thunder through the station."

The small community of Garsdale, some fifty strong, did not seem to care how many trains stopped. "The job of these railwaymen, settled in a compact hamlet amid the scattered hill farms, is to keep the trains rolling. After the line was opened in 1875, sixteen strong stone houses were built by the railway company at Garsdale Station and another half-dozen a few hundred yards away near the Moorcock Viaduct. In them have lived generations of signalmen, gangers and platelayers."

The oldest railwayman in the community was Adam Rudd, who retired at the end of the 1939-45 war. "He has lived at Garsdale for thirty-three years. Now that he is no longer ganger in charge of a long stretch on the Hawes branch line, he has taken on the job of caretaker at the tank house…Winter isolates the Garsdale community. Heavy snows have been known to cut it off from the world for three weeks at a time. The nearest towns are Hawes, six miles to the east, and Sedbergh, ten miles to the west…In the severe winter of 1947 the line was out of action for a month."

The legendary Harold Thwaite, porter, related to the visiting journalist the story of the Great Snow of 1947, a blizzard that was the worst known in living memory. "In a way, Harold is an even older member of the Garsdale community than Adam Rudd, for he was born in a farmhouse within sight of the station fifty-seven years ago, though he did not become a railwayman until 1913…Harold has almost a proprietary interest in the line. His father used to mix the gunpowder used in the blasting operations when cuttings were being driven through the hills…"

Stationmaster Berwick and his wife May had to adjust themselves to an entirely new environment, for his previous post was at Southport. "Mrs Berwick has overcome the first feeling of loneliness and has acclimatised herself to ordering most of her groceries and household goods for fortnightly delivery from Sedbergh. The stone-built houses are solid, comfortable and warm, and Mrs Berwick is happier now that a new tank, which will give the row of cottages running water and bathrooms, is being built up at the station. Up till now all the railway families have depended on one standpipe."

The only member of the Garsdale station community who could not reminisce about railway matters was William Harper, the postmaster.

"He settled there in the post office, which he combines with a tiny general stores, when he got married in 1898. Outside his office is the only telephone kiosk for miles around. It contains the telephone numbered Garsdale Head 1, which has one of those good old wind-em-up handles to call the operator.

"When the old Midland Railway built this lonely outpost town for railwaymen, there was – and there still is – just one local asset. About a mile away is the Moorcock Inn, an old posting house and the only tavern on the sixteen miles of road between Hawes and Sedbergh. There, if the winter week-ends are not too severe, the men can relax after their heavy days keeping the line secure and the water-troughs free from ice.

"For those troughs that replenish the tanks of long-distance trains are the chief worry of the men on top of the Pennines. If they do freeze they have to be cleaned right out and warnings must be flashed up the line. An express which lowered its scoop into ice at sixty miles an hour would hit trouble hard!"

None of the railwayman the journalist met could explain why the daily train from Hawes to Hellifield, which ran through the junction, was known as the Bonnyface. "Mr Berwick's only explanation, gleaned from the old-timers, is that the train was always so punctual that it earned the name as a sort of blessing. Maybe. But if you want to get to Garsdale today, without doing things the hard way, take an express to a nearby express stop station like Appleby and then go by road. It is as remote as that."

In January, 1952, when *BR Magazine* featured Garsdale, the staff comprised six signalmen and two relief signalmen, two porters and a woman crossing keeper (for Grisedale). There were also 40 engineering staff on strength. The Stationmaster was Douglas Cobb and he had the assistance of the indestructable Harold Thwaite.

RAILWAY COTTAGES

There is nothing less like a cottage than the style of "cottage" that the Midland Railway Company built for its "servants." Forget the concept of a cottage as a small, detached building with brightly-painted, shuttered windows, floriferous garden and gateway swathed in honeysuckle. Here were cottages of the terrace variety, built of slate and stone with the object of cheating the Pennine wind and rain.

At t'Junction, where the ground was sloping, there was no single terrace but several short groups of identical houses, pretty enough from the front but unlovely at the rear, where there was a series of yards, each with wash-house, coal-house and outside toilet. A distinctive feature of Midland architecture was the porch, which had two doors and was divided laterally, each porch sheltering the front doors of two houses. Entry was directly into the sitting room.

In addition to the main group of 16 cottages, erected near the station, were Moorcock Cottages, a group of six forming a pretentious block not far from the Moorcock Inn. The western gable end was reinforced with slates, though these dwellings took some shelter from a railway embankment. The end cottage by the station did not have this protection and for a while was damp. All the cottages had roofs of Burlington (Lake District) slates.

With much shift working, and with such a concentration of railway workers, there was always someone wandering about at t'Junction. A signalman was on shift-work. One man went to work at 10 p.m. and finished at 6 am. His relief came off duty at 2 pm, and so on. At any time of day or night there would be a plume of smoke rising from a cottage chimney.

Lighting was by paraffin lamp and/or candle. Margaret Metcalfe recalls there were two paraffin lamps in her family's home, one in the living room and one in the kitchen. She remembers in particular an Aladdin lamp, which had a wick covered by a mantle and a globe to radiate the light. One hung from the ceiling; the other was on a table. "One day, Tommy Airey, the butcher, came in, banged the door, hit the

Aladdin lamp, knocked it to the floor and broke it."

Each cottage had three bedrooms. The mattresses on the beds were usually of goose feathers, being soft and warm. There was also a sitting room and a kitchen with a cast-iron fireplace. Coal for the fire was supplied by Jack Thwaite, who in addition to being a coal merchant had East Clough, a small farm "down at the bottom of the hill." His wife delivered milk.

The coal arrived at the station in wagons and having been transported to his farm was tipped into a large heap. Jack, who supplied good quality coal, using a cart drawn by a horse called Charlie, had coal by the bag or, if half a ton was required, as was the case at the Wilson household, the coal was delivered straight from the railway wagons. "Otherwise, it was only to be carted back up the hill again." With good coal, heating a well designed oven set in the iron fireplace, a housewife at t'Junction had no excuses for poor cooking. She might grumble a little when giving the fireplace its weekly application of black lead.

The side-boiler of the fireplace in the kitchen had to be filled and emptied by hand, using a ladin-can. Out at the back, the wash-house had a boiler and a sink. In addition, there was a mangle, posser and dolly-tub. "Everybody washed on a Monday. I used to go into t'wash-house and put t'fire on under t'set pot. Mother hanged t'clothes on lines on t'Green or between houses."

Given good weather, the clothes dried in an instant. If Garsdale Head was draped with mist as damp as a dish-cloth, or if rain sheeted down as from a celestial tap, the housewife had recourse to a "winter-hedge," a wooden frame that might be placed indoors near the fire. Once dry and ironed, they were usually put to air on a reckon, a wooden rack working from pulleys attached to the ceiling near the fireplace.

The wash-house might also be the venue, for the hardy, when the weekly bath was due. The zinc bath, which usually hung from a hook in the yard, was filled with water heated in the boiler. Otherwise, "we got a tin bath and put it in t'kitchen by t'fire." The family went through the bath in order of seniority – children first, then dad, followed by mother, who had the emptying of the bath and the cleaning up to do.

There was no toilet in the house. One of the facilities at the bottom of the yard was an earth-toilet, which was emptied weekly. A tedious weekly task involved cutting up old newspapers into squares, threading the corners with string and hanging them up behind the door as toilet paper.

Rents were as low as 2s or 3s a week. Amenities were sparse. Richard Fawcett, who in the 1930s was a ganger based on Garsdale, told me of the paraffin lamps that provided light after dark. "Aladdin lamps, we had. Real classy do's…There was only one good lamp in the house and we went upstairs to bed by candlelight." Special lighting was needed for the wash-house across the yard. As mentioned, some people used to bath there as well. "I don't think I ever did bath, as such," said Dick. All my life, I've been damn good at getting in t'river." A pause, and he added: "Even yet."

After years of getting water from "a spout that never froze up," the railway company provided piped water into the houses, having constructed a new reservoir on the hill. The new piped water supply was installed in the early 1950s. A Merrie England aspect was imparted by The Green, where stood posts for washing lines and areas used by quoit-playing railwaymen. The more youthful visitors had games of cricket. When Cyril Breeze was the Stationmaster, he provided the children with a see-saw and swings so The Green continued to be a lively social area.

Margaret Metcalfe, the daughter of Thomas and Rachel Wilson, relates that in 1913, when she was six months old, the family moved from a small rented farm at Lunds to No.1 Cottage at the start of what proved to be a 57 year long association with the place. They were not stay-at-homes. The family went to Carlisle for Christmas shopping. Mrs Wilson, an accomplished dress-maker, got most of her material from Leeds. "Folk were wonderful up yonder at doing things."

At the time the Wilsons lived at No.1, there was a family of Metcalfes at No.2, and Blades at No.3. The Thwaites tenanted No.4, Todds were at No.5 and Rudds at No.6. (Arthur Rudd, son of Adam and Alice Rudd, was born at No.6 and at the time of writing still lives here). Mrs Watson occupied No.7, the Banks family were at No.8, Fields at No.9 and Handleys at No.10. Another family surnamed Metcalfe lived at No.11, John Tom Dawson was at No.12, the Simpsons at No.13 and Feathernhoughs at No.14. Mr Soulsby, the North-Eastern engine driver, and another of North-Eastern connection were at Nos. 15 and 16.

Miss Lilian Thwaite, of No.4, provided teas and bed and breakfast facilities for passengers and others from the 1939-45 war until the late 1970s. Among her guests was the Dutton family of Liverpool. Robin Dutton, a member of the Friends of the Settle-Carlisle Line, writing in the magazine, noted: "It was a ritual for us children, on arriving at Garsdale on the train from Liverpool, via Hellifield, to run to the shop at the bottom of the hill to buy a pencil and notebook to take train numbers during our stay." At this time, Harold Thwaite and his family lived at No.5.

Many years ago, Miss Thwaite told me about the so-called Temperance Hotel, a rather grand title given to No 13 Railway Cottages (as mentioned in Part Three). Mr Reuben Alton, whose home this was, acted as a coal agent. He and his wife provided accommodation mainly for commercial travellers.

When Simon Fothergill was on flagging [cautioning] duty on the line, having neither cabin nor fog hut to shelter him, he contracted pneumonia and died. There was so much sympathy for his widow that any permanent way men who were in need of lodgings were first directed to her home as lodgers. The money she received for bed and breakfast augmented her small income.

When Margaret Wilson was 11 years old, father was promoted and they moved to No.10, and at the age of 21 Margaret married John Metcalfe and left t'Junction for a new home. She still has lively memories of life within a stone's throw of the railway station. Pigs were kept on spare bits of ground. "We never had any more than two pigs. If there were three, someone had joined with him and they had one and a-half pig each." Uncle Ted was one of the pig-killers. Only the squeal was wasted.

"When the pig was dead and hung up, mother caught the blood for black-puddings. She made sausages – a darn sight better than those you buy today." The rest was either eaten immediately or salted down, rolled and slipped on to hooks in the ceiling to dry off for use in the winter.

Moorcock Cottages, which stand high above the road, within easy viewing distance of the famous inn, were described by one railwayman as "wonderful, like palaces compared with what we had in the countryside." They were distinguishable through having wooden floors (which was not the case at t'Junction, where the ground floors were stone-flagged).

There was no piped water. "We had to carry water from a spring under the fourth arch of the viaduct. Being about 200 yards away, it was quite a haul, but everyone had to do it. The chap at the end house emptied the earth closets. I think he got half-a-crown for everyone he emptied and he'd wheel the stuff across the road in a barrow and dump it in the field right opposite. I can remember him taking it 20 or 30 yards up the field and tipping the stuff in heaps for the farmer to spread when he'd time. As soon as a new heap was made, hens would turn up and wallow."

The well-informed article in *John Bull* (1950) mentioned that the rents of the "tied cottages" now owned by British Railways were cheap compared with council houses. "For three-bedroom houses with large downstairs rooms and a separate stone-built outhouse, the average rent is 7s.6d a week, which may rise to 10s when water is installed. Widows and pensioners pay less."

SCHOOL

Most of the local children went to Lunds School. Margaret Wilson, of t'Junction, was one of four – "myself, Maggie Banks, Hetty Rudd, a teacher in the infants' department, and Ted Dawson" - who went on the train to Hawes. "It was a very good school. When we first started going, the headmaster was Henry Bates. He had some scholars who did exceedingly well when he had them in tow. One of the lads at school was Bert Calvert." This was the younger brother of Kit, who was to achieve local fame as the saviour of the Wensleydale cheese-making industry.

The train that conveyed the quartet to school departed at eight o' clock. "Then there was a businessman down Wensleydale who wanted to go to London or somewhere, so they altered the time of the train to 6-20 and we got up and caught that. I had a packed lunch, usually meat sandwiches and cake. At school, a cup of tea was provided for a half-penny. The water was boiled on the premises, using a big kettle on a primus stove. Sometimes I went to an aunt's house at Hawes. I took my packed lunch. She gave me a drink of tea."

The journey to Hawes lasted about a quarter of an hour. "We just waited at the station until it was time for school. Mr Richardson was the Stationmaster. The porters were very good. John Mason used to say to us, drily: 'I know what's been going on at Garsdale; the news percolates down through the mountain crevices.' The duty porter put a fire on in winter. The return train was Bonnyface, at about a quarter to four. My father got me a pass and I think that for three months it cost ten shillings. On a Tuesday, at Hawes station, the cattle docks seemed full of animals that were to be transported in wagons."

In 1924, there were 60 names on the register of Lunds School, which was attended by most of the children from t'Junction and Moorcock cottages, the first-named being about a mile and a-half away. A farmer's daughter who began school in that year recalls that "five-year-old kids were walking to school every day. There was no such thing as a ride."

The teaching staff numbered three - Mr Richardson, headmaster, assisted by his wife and a Miss Akrigg. "We took our own drink and food for the mid-day break. We would have a bottle o' cold tea – they'd be capped [surprised] today – and a few sandwiches, made o' cheese or jam. Just what your mother put up. It wasn't a bad school really cos it had pipes all round. It was more or less centrally heated. You used to put your bottle o' tea o' t'pipe to keep it warm. Before I left, the number of children attending Lunds School had got down to about 40."

For those children crossing the moor from the farms of Grisedale, school was about two miles away. In winter, mothers with lanterns would meet their offspring on the moor to ensure they reached home safely. There was anguish one day when the children missed the path and they and their mothers did not meet at the appointed place at the appointed time.

Pat Brown, born in 1929, began to attend school when his family was at the big lodge on Mossdale Estate. He had a walk of almost two miles to attend Lunds school, which he did until he was 14 years of age. "It was a busy little school, with two teachers – the headmaster and a junior teacher. At the start, we used slates for writing – there was a squeaky sound as we worked - and then they gradually introduced pencils and paper." He remembers that when Mr Grainger from Hawes was the headmaster, and about 30 children were on the register, a school trip by train was organised. There was great excitement as they were conveyed down the Wensleydale line on the way to Redcar for a day out at the seaside.

Arthur Rudd recalls that he and other children had to walk a mile to school at Lunds. They walked in all weathers. "Wet or fine - we had to go, just the same." It was the period when Mr Grainger was the head. Hetty Rudd was the only other teacher. (When she married, she became Hetty Thompson).

By the 1950s, buses were taking schoolchildren to school. Few children of school age lived at Garsdale Head.

CHURCH AND CHAPEL

Before the 1939-45 war, the down platform waiting room also served as a church. The parish church was at a distance of several miles, so consideration was given to the Garsdale Headers. The waiting room was about 30 ft long and 10 ft wide, illuminated by oil lamps. The service was usually held on a Sunday morning and the ministry of the Rev Badrick is well remembered.

Local folk subscribed towards the cost of a harmonium, which has been described as "an ill wind that nobody blows any good." It was kept in one of the cottages and just before service time two men carried it to the place of worship. A visiting journalist wrote of the strains of the hymns being drowned by the howling of the wind sweeping down from the fells. There survives in the area at least one copy of the Book of Common Prayer marked: "Hawes Junction Waiting Room Service," dated October, 1920, with the injunction "Not to be taken away."

Margaret Metcalfe recalls: "There were maybe six or seven of us. In winter, a fire was lit in the grate. I quite well remember that before we had the harmonium, Mrs Watson, a signalman's wife, played the violin for the hymn-signing. Then she went to live at Scotby." It was on the harmonium that Margarent learnt how to play Church music – "the Magnificat and the Nunc Dimittis and such like." Maggie Banks was also a proficient organ-player. The Gamsbys of Grisedale Crossing, added their voices to that of the small congregation.

The *Daily Express* in 1937 sent a photographer and reporter to Garsdale to attend a service. A photograph showed group of worship-pers, including Jenny Banks, daughter of the Stationmaster, with the caption: "They sing hymns as trains roar by." The reporter began his story: "Carrying a little black bag containing miniature Communion plate and vestments, Garsdale's sturdy, smiling vicar, the Rev F G Badrick, walked tonight up the steep approach to the railway station at Garsdale Head, lonely hillside hamlet at the extreme end of his scat-tered parish."

The reporter from the *Express* joined women, children and a railway signalman in the tiny waiting room. "The platform was deserted except for the sudden roar of a train on its way to Scotland, quickly fading into the hills. Then dim organ music came from the waiting-room. Women's voices sang a hymn. The monthly Church of England service in this remote North Yorkshire hamlet had begun."

Mrs Wilson, wife of a railway foreman, who distributed the hymn books, had laid a cloth over a small table that served as an altar. The Bishop had given permission for Communion to be celebrated. A lectern was the only other furniture in the oil-lit waiting-room. They sang with vigour, standing in front of railway posters advertising holiday resorts. "Their voices carried across the valley, the narrow River Clough running through it, to the fells beyond."

It was almost 50 years since permission was first given to hold Sunday services in Garsdale Station waiting-room. First they were held fortnightly, then monthly. In 1945, the waiting room-cum-church still contained the harmonium and "a few moth-eaten hymn books." By 1950, the services were almost forgotten and the harmonium had gone for firewood.

Frederick George Badrick (1875-1952) was the last incumbent of Garsdale who had the parish as his sole cure. His tenure extended from 1923 until his death. An insight into the station services is provided by his Diary. On Psalm Sunday, 1934, he wrote: "In the evening I had the Junction [station] service. The day was a full one with two celebrations and a rather long gospel. One of my loyal supporters there is Mr Brown, a gamekeeper from Moorland Cottage. He has a long walk coming by the most direct way along the branch line."

Mr Badrick added that the gamekeeper had enjoyed reading a book the Vicar had loaned him. This was the biography of Dr Wilson, who achieved fame, having been with Scott in the Antarctic. The Vicar wrote that he had passed on the book to him "owing to Wilson's work on grouse disease. Brown, while reading, suddenly discovered he was reading the life of the author whose grouse book is in the library of the shooting box."

The folk of Dent once said: "We wouldn't grow rhubarb in Gasd'l." An element of rivalry existed between Garsdale and the neighbouring parish of Lunds. When preaching on St Bartholomew's Day, 1947, Mr Badrick amused the Garsdale congregation. Seeking to point to the relevance of the verse, "Can anything good come out of Nazareth?" (John 1 v 46), he added mischievously, "...as one might say, 'Can anything good come out of Lunds'?" The benefice of Lunds was united with that of Hardraw on May 7, 1858. Before that time, it was a separate chapelry.

Lunds Church, by the headwaters of the river Ure, was referred to by

The Yorkshire Post in the 1930s as the Loneliest Church in Wensleydale. Situated about six miles from Hawes, it was stated to be the smallest church in the Diocese of Ripon. Light for Lunds came from two windows and the heat from two paraffin stoves. There was no vestry, no chancel, no tower and no porch.

The furnishings consisted of two rows of seats divided by an aisle, the seating capacity being sixty people. A small American organ, an altar and lectern were among the furnishings. In the north-east corner was a reading desk that also served as a pulpit. A single bell was situated in a tiny turret. "About a score of tombstones in the churchyard are the only features which would enable a stranger to distinguish it at a distance from numerous hay barns in the vicinity."

Incredibly, it is held that Handel's *Messiah* was once performed in the church. The Misses Holmes, three Lancashire ladies, tenanted Clough Cottage at Garsdale Head from 1925-68 and kept it as a much appreciated Dales retreat. They happened to attend Lunds Church at a time when Mr Macfie was a member of the congregation.

R A Scott Macfie, a good-looking and sophisticated bachelor, was the dominant figure at Lunds from his arrival here just after the 1914-18 war to his death in 1935. A member of a family of sugar-refiners in Liverpool, Macfie became a dalesman by adoption. He converted Shaws, a high-lying farmhouse, into a home and here he began to develop an estate. An imposing stone gateway led into a drive giving access to Lunds church. The gateway and drive were built at the instructions of Mr Macfie. The Rev J Howard, Vicar of Hardraw, writing in 1930, stated that the former approach was "across fields that are boggy in the extreme, except in seasons of drought."

There was never an easy way to Shaws, Macfie's home, which stood on the 1,000 ft contour. Macfie was worried about the isolation. "Above me is the old packhorse highway that passes over Hell Gill bridge and connects Wensleydale with Brough...All my friends are poachers." For a time, he rented a cottage by the main road, regarding it as a place where he could live whenever he was ill. He wrote in 1931: "My sister will arrive in an hour at Hawes Junction and I don't know how to convey her and her bags to Shaws."

At Shaws, Macfie attempted to forget the trauma of wartime and the loss of many good friends. An Anglican, he provided Lunds with a harmonium of unusual design. When not in use, it might be folded, wrapped in canvas and strapped. He was never in good health. In 1931, he wrote: "I shall have to be careful for the rest of my mis-spent life and be prohibited from walking uphill – a comic suggestion to a dweller at Lunds."

He none the less did much good work on behalf of the local farming community. Macfie was to be long remembered if only for his celebratory bonfires and Christmas parties. One of the farming families invited him to be godfather to their son. Mr Badrick mentioned Macfie in his 1935 diary, noting: "He has taken a great deal of pains in discovering the early beginnings of Lunds Church. Recently, there has been a revision of the boundaries of Hardraw and Lunds...An Order in Council has been obtained on conditions which Macfie finds to be invalid. He thinks the process should be withdrawn and some national re-arrangement made to provide for its greater independence...He seems to think the powers-that-be in Ripon Diocese are strangely indifferent to the vital needs of that remote corner of the Diocese."

Ill-health caused him to lose some of his good humour. "It is a bore to go on living; and if there were no fog, I should console myself by sitting at a window to gaze affectionately at Lunds churchyard. I have a devastating cold and my eyes feel like misfits." In 1935, the Jubilee year of King George V, Mr Macfie paid men to carry combustible material on to the high ground between Grisedale Crossing and the dale itself, so there might be a bonfire worthy of remembrance. It was the last of many notable occasions in his life at Lunds. When he died soon afterwards, he was buried in the yard of that little church at which he had gazed while at Shaws.

The coffin, draped with the Union Jack, was placed on a cart drawn by his old horse Deborah. Twenty or thirty dalesmen, crow-black in their funeral garb, were in the company of mourners. One was heard to say: "Why, that's auld Deborah. Many's the time he told me as how he liked her that much that, if she died, he'd put up a tombstone for her. An' now, he's gone first." On his funeral day, many gipsies were present, for he had been a leading figure in the Gipsy Lore Society.

The church was so small that the coffin was laid across the chancel. Sheep now lie on the sun-warmed gravestone. When a young man from a local farm died, his sorrowing mother arranged with the landowner – for the church was no longer in use – that her son, who revered Macfie, might be buried beside him. She was sure they would have plenty of interesting things to talk about.

Pat Brown, whose father was churchwarden at Lunds Church for many years, told me of the time when to reach the building it was necessary to negotiate the infant Ure on planks, one plank stretching to a small island and the other extending from here to the far bank. Those who used it had the benefit of a handrail on one side. (There is now a good footbridge).

Parsons who served Lunds included Henry Waterton, who was at Hardraw. He was transported to Lunds Church for the services by taxi, a big Rover car, owned and usually driven by Tom Allen of Hawes. Pat recalls: "He also picked up father and when I was a lad I sometimes joined them for the trip to Lunds. My father rang the one little bell – it was a straight pull."

Garsdale was a Methodist valley, and the Methodists had the sort of faith that would move mountains. "The [Anglican] Church didn't have many people at one time. Only about three used to go, but it managed to keep going. It's much better now." Primitive Methodists met weekly at Mount Zion Chapel, a modest building of which a minister wrote: "Lack of money, linked with a conviction to build, has produced a simple, honest building that can hold its head up against some of the more florid structures of the period." The Chapel dates from 1876, which was the year the Settle-Carlisle was opened for regular passenger trains.

The land on which the chapel was built had been bought from a Skipton wine merchant for £5. Reuben Alton, who had the so-called Temperance Hotel at one of the railway cottages, laid a foundation stone. Eventually, the Altons migrated "Leeds way" but when Reuben died he was interred at Garsdale Smithy chapel. Among the first worshippers at Mount Zion were farmers, two labourers and a stonemason. The Pratt family, cattle-dealers, supported the chapel. Richard Bell Pratt and his brother, Matthew Slinger Pratt, bought the organ in memory of their father, the indomitable Willie Pratt.

In the 1930s, there were Good Friday Tea Parties, with a smoky brazier out-of-doors to heat water for the big teapots. On Anniversary Day, the Sunday School scholars had the nerve-jangling experience of standing up in front of a crowd of people to recite or sing. "We all took our own mugs and in the afternoon we had tea. At night they had a service and a supper for everybody." One of the Pratt family cooked a big ham and took it to the chapel to be used for sandwiches.

Conditions might be cramped for special services, the chapel consisting of a single room. Viewers of a notable television documentary were aware of this when the chapel was the setting for a service taken by an old-time evangelist, Herbert Silverwood, who had been "packing 'em in" at chapels in the Dales for many years.

One Good Friday, over 100 people found places within, listening to a lusty "message" and then tucking in to supper. The company could eat as much as they liked for 60p a head. A rib-stretching supper has been a feature of the Chapel Anniversary. When Sedbergh Circuit held a family service here, so many people turned up that some of them spent the afternoon out-of-doors.

Well remembered is Mrs Jennie Thornborrow. She and her husband were farming in Grisedale until he became a railway signalman at Garsdale. On his death, she carried on an energetic association with the Chapel that had begun in 1943. When I chatted with her in 1984, she was a Methodist local preacher and, at Mount Zion, the organist, Sunday School teacher, treasurer, caretaker and steward. Some years had gone by since the chapel reverberated to a Love Feast, a service of testimony during which water and biscuits were passed around.

In the 1930s were held an annual Camp Meeting and Love Feast, at one of which 70 people gave their testimonies. At about this time, Jennie Thornborrow's grandmother – a Lund from Brough Sowerby –

expressed a wish to attend. Relatives tried to discourage her, for she was old and they felt the journey might be too far for her. She quietly insisted on going. The only available seat was behind a partition. She saw nothing – and spent the next day in bed, exhausted. "We told you it would be too much for you," said one of the family. "Aye," said Grannie, "but I'se bin."

At t'Junction cottages, I heard that a God-fearing family would attend chapel on a Sunday afternoon and "entertain ourselves" on a Sunday night. This consisted of a gathering round the piano to sing such songs as The Old Rugged Cross and "no end of Ranter hymns." The folk next door opened their door. The sound of piano and singing with gusto carried from one living room to the next.

The voices of the Garsdale Singers were raised in Dales chapels for at least thirty years, up to 1966. They occasionally rendered their much-loved programme of sacred songs at Mount Zion, Garsdale Head. The core members were children of Roland and Mary Jane Bracken. Roland died in September, 1945, and Mary Jane in 1960, when she was aged 92 years. Members of the group were Jack and Jenny Bracken (Low Scale), Nellie and Tom Peacock, Jinny and George Mason (The Street), Willie and Hilda Bracken (Cote Weggs), Bob and Agnes Bracken (Paradise).

THE LIBRARY

A visitor to Garsdale in 1938, when the Stationmaster was J F Ferguson, noted that one need never be afraid of a long wait at this station. "If it is in the daytime – and if you have an honest face – you can go into the waiting room and perhaps the Stationmaster will lend you a book from the unique library there."

At about the turn of the century, some 150 books were presented to the station. The donor was a lady living in Wensleydale who had often used the station. She felt sorry for the railwaymen who lived miles from anywhere. The books were given into the charge of Mr Ferguson. He therefore added to his duties as Stationmaster those of chief librarian.

Many of the books were of the Victorian "improving" kind.

The librarian's register – an old ruled exercise book – held a faded letter, dated March 5, 1906, from Mrs Greenwood, of Bedale, addressed to Mr Bunce, Stationmaster of Hawes Junction, stating that the Religious Tract Society was sending a bundle of books and that she herself was adding two more parcels. The books were to be loaned free of charge to the staff. The library was also reported to be "a welcome diversion for railway officials whose duties have brought them to Garsdale for a few hours."

This private library was housed in the up platform ladies' waiting-room. Reginald Berwick, the Stationmaster in 1950, took the representative of *John Bull* into the waiting-room and unlocked the glass fronted cupboards in which the books were being kept. The range of reading material was wide, with Dickens, Scott and Jules Verne well represented. There were some bound Chambers's Journals, Whitaker's Almanack for 1908, two copies of *Motley's Rise of the Dutch Republic*, and a novel entitled *Patience Hart's First Experience in Service*.

Mr Berwick, in 1950, was reported to have said: "Nobody asks to borrow books from this little library now, though they are always available. I have read a good many of them myself in the three years I have been here. Now the county library sends books round, they all go for the more modern stuff." In due course, modern fiction was added. In 1945, when Daniel May was the Stationmaster, the library was still "spick and span."

TANK HOUSE

The space beneath the huge iron tank that dispensed water to the columns on the platforms serving the North East and Midland lines achieved a special sort of fame. It became the local palais de danse, the cinema and the concert hall. From about 1918 until the coming of television caused interest in rural socials to dwindle, Garsdalians used the lofty room as a social centre.

Here were held domino and whist drives, potato pie suppers and concerts. The Tank House would take 50 or 60 people at a pinch and was used for dances, parties and chapel socials. "Many a merry wedding or birthday party was held there."

Two big coal-burning stoves kept the place warm in winter. Walls made of dressed stone supported the iron tank with a capacity of 80,000 gallons of water. "When you were in the Tank House, you didn't know the water was there; it didn't make a noise or anything. The water was used to feed the engines. They had a reservoir in a quarry-hole yonder which fed the station and also the cottages. Here there was an open spout that was never known to freeze up."

Margaret Metcalfe remembers the days when the Tank House had a flagged floor. There was occasionally dancing on the flags but the Garsdalers held back until they got a wooden floor. A dance held in the school raised £25. They had already fitted a "tin" roof beneath the tank, making the room less lofty and forbidding. Now, with the proceeds of the dance they could buy enough boards for a floor, a gramophone, a piano, lamps and many other objects.

The floorboards were purchased cheaply at Gretna Green when, just after the 1914-18 war, old Army huts were being dismantled. Margaret

Metcalfe remembers that her father, Thomas Wilson, and George Fretwell, a signalman, went up to Gretna with cash in their pockets and the idea of buying floorboards for the Tank House.

Margaret recalls when a wedding party was held there. "I was only very small at the time when Betsy Blades – Auntie Bessy, we called her - married George Parsley at Garsdale Church and they had a party there. Auntie Bessy was in a white dress with a veil. A table had been set right up the middle of the Tank House. The meal was a knife and fork affair. There was bound to be some ham."

When dances were held, "from eight till twelve," Mrs Curtis, a teacher at Lunds was one of the regular visiting musicians. Anyone who could play a musical instrument was welcome to join in. Some of the Tank House events raised up to £40 for the Bradford Royal Infirmary. Such dances were known as "Bradford do's." Monetary gifts to the hospital were a form of "thank you" because in the 1930s trains were stopped to rush emergencies for operations to Bradford.

The station dances attracted people "from all over." "T'biggest part of 'em came on bikes. Others walked." Those living in the neighbouring dale of Dent used the Coal Road as a handy, if rough and exposed, cycle route – a four mile return journey twixt the stations of Dent and Garsdale. "Then, at Dent, in t'wee small hours, they might have another couple of miles to go to where they lived."

At the Tank House, the wallflowers [non-dancers] sat on red-upholstered seats that had been taken from a scrapped railway carriage of Midland ancestry; "there was always a dive to get the best seats." The refreshment room was a coach "that came off the North-East," sporting its original doors. "They brought that coach by rail, used jacks and sleepers and shoved it into position...At dances, it was a recognised thing among t'older lads to take their lady friends through into t'old railway coach for supper."

Inside were long tables and some chairs. "There was a bit of a kitchen at one end, a coke stove and a boiler used for heating water. It held between four and five gallons. We warmed up water for tea. Just tea. Members of the committee brought the food. It was mainly sandwiches

– ham sandwiches, beef sandwiches – any sort of sandwiches – and always plenty of cakes. And even trifles…Sometimes, we had tatie pies."

The railway company, in a fit of generosity, ran a water supply from the main tank into the supper room. Tea was "mashed" in a big teapot and there were both cups and saucers. The tea-cups rattled when the expresses went thundering by, a few yards away. "There were no toilets – just 'outside' – but the sheep didn't care."

Before the coach-cum-refreshment room was put in place, a long table was set up at one end of the Tank House. The place was always cheerfully decorated. The floor is remembered as being like a skating rink at times. The tongue-and-groove boarding bought at Gretna Green covered a layer of sleepers "You couldn't wish for a better floor for dancing Waltzes and Three Steps and Lancers. "All the lot of 'em."

Margaret, who was one of the pianists, recalls that one or two local people had pianos in their homes. Someone would lend a piano for a "do" at the Tank House. Maggie Banks, the Stationmaster's daughter, was on hand to play. "After we left, 'Bel Gamsby [Isobel Gamsby, from Grisedale Crossing] would do it." Another pianist with a lively manner was Alice Scarr, of The Moorcock. Eventually it was possible to have a small band, with perhaps two accordionists and a drummer. One former dancer says: "I've been there when everyone who was dancing was black-wet wi' sweat." Concerts with local artistes took place in winter.

Mr Cobb, the Stationmaster who played the accordion for the dancing complained that most of the farmers and their wives would only consider "olde-tyme" dances; they "won't look at the samba and modern stuff, perhaps because we have not enough young people to set an example." A former signalman recalled: "When we came here, in 1934, the Tank House dances were attended by farm folk and railway folk. There was little else to do at Garsdale at the time. They were good dances. Everybody joined in the Sixpenny Hops (Tanner 'ops)."

Harry Cockerill squeezed many a lively tune from his accordion. Harry had grown up in a lonely old farmstead at the head of Langstrothdale. He was a self-taught piano accordionist who chuckled when he said that there had been no close neighbours to upset when he was practising. At first, attending functions, he travelled by motor bike, with his accordion fastened to the pillion seat with cow-bands. When Pat Brown's wife, Sheila, had her 21st birthday party in the Tank House, the music for dancing was provided by a band from Settle.

In the inter-war years, Inspector Harry Swain stood out above all others as the most paternal supervisor. He visited the concerts and get-togethers. He smoothed the passage of little ventures, such as the transport of a favourite piano from Grisedale Crossing to the concert room under the Tank at Garsdale station.

When Adam Rudd met Eric Bennett, a writer for *John Bull*, in December, 1950, they waited until an express freight train had roared along the up track to the water troughs, then crossed the rails. In the case of Adam Rudd, this was with the dignity that became his seventy-six years. Adam opened the door of the Tank House with his key. "The great metal tank, with its thousands of gallons of water for the locomotive cranes, stood above the normal tall, stone building which you can see in any railway station yard. But when Adam Rudd stepped through the door, it was not into a workshop. Along the white-washed walls stood four long settees in red-and-black patterned plush, which on closer inspection were recognisable as the seats from an old-style Midland Railway saloon coach.

"Rows of chairs were in the body of the hall, and the floor showed signs of having been polished for dancing. At the far end of the tank house was a stage with gaily-coloured chintz curtains. Two stoves were installed to keep the lofty room warm on nights when the snows sweep down from the fells. 'Aye,' said Adam, with a quiet smile of satisfaction on his rugged face. 'This is where we have our little do's. Ah've moved piano to welfare centre to keep the damp from getting at it'."

The tank house, with the roof beneath the tank strengthened as special protection, was described in *John Bull* as "the heart of life on winter evenings...In the tank house the floor may be cleared for a dance or the local talent giving a concert from the stage, while the stoves defy the snowflakes." "We make our own amusements here," says Adam.

"Always have done."

Adam's son, Arthur, was caretaker at the Tank House. He was the one who made the fires in the two big coal stoves, using fuel provided for the purpose by the railway company. He also tidied up when a social event was over. It was also Arthur's job to keep an eye on the big tank and ensure that plenty of water was available.

In 1953, a representative of *The Northern Echo*, visiting Garsdale's novel dance hall noticed it had a tiny stage and a good space for dancing. "The walls are pleasantly decorated in white. Multi-coloured tinsel stars hang in festoons from the roof. Here, to the strains of Stationmaster Cobb's accordion, the folk from the fells dance on many a winter's night...These dances at Garsdale are such warm, happy affairs, with the stoves going strong...that the railway gang never have to worry about the water tank freezing."

The topic of Tank House dances was elaborated in The Upper Wensleydale Newsletter (March, 1997), after the senior-citizens had been invited to recall their experiences. Sometimes, they would have to walk there and back – from Hawes, Bainbridge, Askrigg, Stalling Busk, Garsdale and down Mallerstang. The girls from Grisedale came in wellies with their dance shoes in a bag. A girl from afar was lucky if she managed to get a lift on a lad's motor-bike. Sometimes there were three on a bike. Those dancers who arrived on push-bikes usually left them at the weighbridge beside the road leading up to the station.

"It wasn't exactly posh! There was water running down the walls. It was a bit makeshift. When they spun you round in the reels you'd end up under the seats!" Mark and Harold Hammond, of Askrigg, were recalled as "brilliant dancers." No one thought of stopping at twelve; sometimes it could be two or even four o'clock in the morning before the dance ended. "They'd come round with the hat for money to keep the band going for an extra hour."

Patrons of the Tank House dances were to remember Mr Cobb, the Stationmaster, and Micky Walker, who when not accompanying dances was presiding over a fish and chip shop at Askrigg. He could "play anything." Osmond Bradbury, from Fell End, beyond Sedbergh, was nicknamed Strauss. He was proficient at the banjo, saxophone and drums. Osmond was a member of the Gaiety Band from Kirkby Stephen. Beresford's Band came to Garsdale from the head of Wharfedale. Alderson Metcalfe, who had no feet and moved about in a three-wheeled invalid chair, played the mouth organ expertly.

The Tank House was demolished in 1971. Margaret Metcalfe says: "I don't know what they pulled it down for. It was a historic building. The stones were all dressed, you know."

POST OFFICE AND SHOP

William Hodgson Harper, a big, smart man with a prominent moustache, was awarded the BEM for his half century of service as Sub Postmaster at Garsdale Head. As a shopkeeper, he sold almost everything, including groceries, sweets and tobacco, known locally as "baccy." An ounce of baccy, brown twist, cost thruppence. "Some people chewed black twist and spit it out." The Harpers also retailed oatmeal, lemonade, cough mixture, brooms and fire shovels. "If you kept a few hens, you went and got a hundredweight of corn." He was also a newsagent, paying special attention to the local newspapers – to the *Craven Herald*, *Westmorland Gazette* and *Cumberland and Westmorland Herald*.

T H (Tommy) Harper, recalling his early days at Garsdale Head when we met in 1971, said that when he was young he climbed out of bed early on a Wednesday morning. His father kept the local shop. Before going to school at Lunds, he helped father to weigh out bags of yeast, which were distributed in the dale early on the traditional baking day.

Father kept the shop that stood at the approaches to Garsdale station. He was also, for 57 years, the sub-postmaster at Garsdale Head. Mail for Garsdale was railborne to Lowgill, where it was dropped into nets, the express not stopping for a moment in its headlong rush to Scotland. From Lowgill, mail was taken to Sedbergh by horse and trap. Deliveries to the head of Garsdale were undertaken by a cycling postman.

Father had a horse and cart with which to take provender to the farms and parcels to Hawes on market day. Paraffin was delivered to him in wooden barrels, consigned by rail. Each barrel contained 50 gallons. In the 1930s, father was supplied with petrol in two-gallon cans, the petrol being retailed to motorists.

Among the memories of Miss Edna Isabella Harper (1913-Sept 10, 1996), who took over the shop on the death of her father, was delivering the mail over the fell to Grisedale. Edna, who was born in the house at the bottom of the Coal Road – within sight and hearing of Garsdale station and its heavy rail traffic – was one of seven children, five of them boys. One boy died in childhood; the other four working for the Settle-Carlisle. Tommy, whom I knew best, was a ganger at Aisgill and Garsdale.

Edna presided at an old-fashioned wooden counter over which had been tacked some American cloth. Dozens of objects were to be seen hanging from hooks driven into the rafters and ceiling. The Misses Holmes, who tenanted a cottage at Garsdale head and visited it for holidays, went into Edna's shop and were thrilled to see some old-fashioned stone water bottles needed for airing beds in the days before electric blankets. A succession of friends enjoyed holidays at Clough Cottage, returning year after year.

"A great treat for our children when on holiday was to be able to visit Edna's shop for sherbert lemons and gipsy cream biscuits." In the days when water for domestic purposes was laboriously transported from a pump at the station, it was not unknown for Edna, having made an effort to fill a bucket, to struggle with it back to the shop. If anyone was in need of water – such as hikers, calling at the shop on a hot day - she would share with them her precious reserve. Edna, though hard of hearing, knew what was going on.

Edna was a familiar figure behind the counter in the family shop. In a tribute to her published in the Friends of the Settle-Carlisle Line magazine it was said that each Christmas she would write letters to 60 people in various parts of the world. Infirmity led her to give up the Post Office on the death of her parents, but she continued to run the shop, selling sweet and groceries, often at cost. One of her customers remarked: "Edna's shop-keeping was more a social or charitable activity than a financial practice." The Spar grocers in Hawes would bring her goods that she sold at very little profit to herself but for the convenience of local people.

A story of Edna concerns a visit by her cousin Hetty. The two ladies went on the train to Carlisle. They waited for the return train on what proved to be the wrong platform and found they had missed the last stopping train. The express was due to leave. The driver saw these two stranded passengers and said: "Eh! Are you Edna Harper?" He had known the Harper brothers in the days when he was a fireman on the line. "Come on, lasses," he said, "I'll get you home." The express stopped at Garsdale station to allow Edna and cousin Hetty to alight. (The only other personage for whom the express was known to stop was – the Prince of Wales!).

Edna was interred at Low Smithy chapel. Two poignant hymns sung by a large congregation were Abide with Me and The Day Thou Gavest.

THE MOORCOCK

Standing where the Hawes-Sedbergh road is joined by the highway from Kirkby Stephen is The Moorcock, named after the red grouse and first mentioned in relation to the railway when Frederick Williams called here when collecting material for his history of the Midland Railway.

He wrote that "travellers innumerable have been wont to dismount their mountain ponies at The Moorcock to refresh themselves with mountain dew." Perhaps they did this "the more willingly from the thought that it has been many a mile since they had such an opportunity before, and that it will be many another before they will have one again."

The Moorcock was the venue, on the afternoon of Boxing Day, 1910 of the preliminary inquiry into the Christmas Eve accident between

Hawes Junction and Aisgill. That was exceptional. Usually, it catered for local people and those on holiday. Some families travelled to Garsdale by train and stayed at the inn for a fortnight. Among them were anglers with an interest in the headwaters of the Ure.

PART SIX

At t'Junction Today

The actual condition of the infrastructure on the
Settle-Carlisle line is at the highest level it has been
since the early 80s, with £1.6 million spent
annually on maintenance alone.

Richard Fearn, of Railtrack, 1999

The Settle-Carlisle hums with activity. Sprinters operated by Northern Spirit, maintain an improved Leeds-Carlisle passenger service. With integrated rail and bus services, and walks based on railway stations being led by cheerful volunteers, rail users have the opportunity of exploring a wide swathe of dale-country. At the remaining stations, buildings have been renovated and painted. When Appleby had received the costly treatment, it was the turn of Garsdale's platforms and structures to be updated.

Greater usage of the passenger service occurred with a concessionary, wintertime £2 fare, available to anyone holding a Dales Railcard and living within local postal districts. At times it was "standing room only" for some. Time-keeping is generally good but some complaints were made about the occasional grimy state of carriage windows. Passengers were trying to see the dale-country through "a glass darkly." On the Settle-Carlisle, the view is everything.

There is magic in the name Settle-Carlisle which attracts ever more people thanks largely to Media coverage. Television in particular brings a swift and satisfying response to those concerned with tourism. When the BBC turned a camera on the Settle-Carlisle line for one of its travel shows, the Tourist Information Centre at Settle was promptly swamped with enquiries.

The track itself is to have an investment of £15 million over the next three years. Further funding is expected in the following seven years, leading to continuously welded rail track along much of the 72 miles from Settle to Carlisle. The new welded rail should offer greater reliability and increased passenger comfort. Commercially, it will also enable the system to cope with increased freight traffic, using heavier trains.

SOUNDS OF GARSDALE

Garsdale station echoes with train sounds as heavy freight trains and stock diverted from the Lancaster-Carlisle thunder through. "Steam specials" usually stop here for water. At other times, the sounds of Garsdale are natural sounds, including the calls of moor birds.

Margaret Metcalfe, who was reared in a railway family at t'Junction told me how local people grew accustomed to the traffic, which once was at the rate of 90 trains a day. "When you lived there, you never noticed the steam trains. Except an express like the Stranraer to Nottingham. You always noticed that. It came through at two o' clock in the afternoon. I think some people set their clocks by it. The Grisedale farmers did. They could see it."

When I involuntarily spent one and a-half hours at Garsdale station last March, I was impressed by the absence of sound and noticed that here, as on most other rural stations, there is no regular staff. I arrived in good time, so that – as a Garsdale friend remarked – I might "soak up the atmosphere." That evening, at an elevation of around 1,000 ft, a chilling breeze was delivering sleet, which came down at an angle of 45 degrees.

The station was being restored. New platform edges had been fitted. The as yet unimproved waiting room was dark, cold and cheerless, so I found bield [shelter] in the lee of the toilet block. After all, the train would be arriving in 20 minutes. If there are ghosts at t'Junction, they were not in the mood to materialise. No one else was at the station that night. The denizens of the railway cottages were housebound. If there were sheep on the hill, they were not giving their positions away by bleating.

A grey day degenerated into nocturnal gloom. The signal box, now closed for most of the time, was as lifeless as a garden shed. Mentally, I brought it back to life, installing a cheery fire and a pipe-smoking signalman. The cosy scene faded; the signal box resumed its lack-lustre appearance. I stared down the track to where three semaphore signals maintained the fixed, stiff posture of old servants who were rarely needed.

The only lights to break the Garsdale gloom were in strings, draping the toilet block, like Christmas decorations someone had forgot to take down, and the odd light further long the platform. Sleet turned to snowflakes that fluttered like butterflies in a pool of yellow light.

Half an hour later, I took a turn along the platform to ease my creaking legs. Light from the former railway cottages seeped across the new platforms. A distant rumbling could only be a train, about to emerge from cover near the Moorcock Cottages and little Mount Zion chapel, then making a dash for Dandry Mire viaduct. The locomotive fixed me with unblinking headlights. Someone had forgotten to switch on the carriage lights. Or so I thought until the train roused the echoes of the station as it thundered through. One of the tireless gypsum trains was taking empty containers back to Drax power station for a re-fill.

By now, there was nothing I could see beyond my pool of light than the blocky form of the hill above the station, whence cometh the station water supply. When the Sprinter arrived, an hour late, I was told it had been delayed by a flooded track near Carlisle. Thankfully, I stepped into a warm, brightly-lit carriage and left Garsdale to the snow. The platforms looked as though they had been powdered with icing sugar. The only marks on the pristine whiteness were made by the soles of my boots.

A WENSLEYDALE UPDATE

Towards the end of 1998, the Wensleydale Railway Association launched a community bus, to link Garsdale and Northallerton, anticipating the return of a regular rail service between the two places – a restored line that would connect the Settle-Carlisle with the East Coast Main Line.

The WRA, formed in 1990, and supported by over 2,000 members, is determined to restore the 40-mile line and create the longest restored railway in the land. Experience of running a bus service was gained in the summer of 1998, with an open-top bus service, named the Wensleydale Tourer, connecting Garsdale and Aysgarth.

An editorial in *Relay*, the WRA magazine, for February, 1999, deals with the successful introduction of the WRC's summer bus service in upper Wensleydale and adds: "Since than, we have been awarded a contract by the County Council to run a more extensive service through the winter. So, you may ask, are we giving up trains in favour of buses? Most certainly not. Buses are a stepping stone on our journey towards an integrated transport system in Wensleydale, centred around the railway."

For 18 miles, between Garsdale and Redmire, the route is trackless and several bridges have been removed. The estimated cost of restoration is £1 million a mile. For 22 miles, from Redmire to Northallerton, the track is in place. It was used until 1992 for transporting lime from quarries at Redmire. I witnessed the slow passage of a special passenger train up the branch when the freight service had ended. It was foggy, imparting a sense of mystery. The fog cleared during the stop at Redmire, when the area swarmed with passengers and onlookers. Then, as the special train cleared the station, and three fog-detonators gave it a distinctive railway farewell, the fog closed in again.

Four years after the mineral traffic ended, the Ministry of Defence took over the line, spent £750,000 on it and used it to move heavy military vehicles from Catterick Camp to the Army range. Following discussions with the Ministry of Defence, the WRA will be able to operate over the line, though the track must be upgraded for passenger traffic.

Meanwhile, at Hawes, the station adjacent to the Dales Countryside Museum has track, platforms, restored building and an industrial tank engine, skilfully transformed into the type of locomotive that worked the last Northallerton-Hawes train in 1954. The locomotive is attached to three coaches with a "blood-and-custard" livery.

Appendices

1: Location of Railway Workers and Households in 1871: Garsdale

Address	Householder/Age	Occupation	Born	Number in H/H	Rly Wkrs
Dandragarth	William Cowper 27	Rly Labourer	Garsdale	4	1
Cockbrow	William S Walmey 32	Civil Engineer	London	2	1
Town Green Huts	Cooper William 43	Rly Labourer	Leicestershire	11	8
Town Green Huts	Welch James 33	Rly Labourer	Petersfield	4	3
Town Green Huts	William Jackson 33	Rly Labourer	Norfolk	13	8
Town Green Huts	Edward Gilbert 28	Rly Labourer	Plymouth	11	5
Town Green Huts	James Jackson 46	Stone Mason	Kendal	10	4
Town Green Huts	Edward Fawcett 35	Rly Labourer	Martin, Lancs	11	6
Town Green Huts	Henry Greene 45	Rly Labourer	Lancs	18	6
Crosthwaite Cottage	?? Welch 25	Sub-Contractor	NK	5	1
Raygill Huts	Charles Walker 37	Rly Engineer	Matlock, Derbs	12	6
Raygill Huts	Charles Burdell 49	Carpenter	Northants	10	5
Raygill Huts	George Gibb 30	Rly Miner	Gloucester	12	7
Raygill Huts	Samuel Roberts40	Bricklayer	London	13	8
Raygill Huts	Thomas Seale 40	Rly Labourer	Northants	13	7
Raygill Huts	Thomas Jeffrey 49	Rly Labourer	Staffs	11	7
Raygill Huts	James Hart 42	Housekeeper	Cambridgeshire	12	10
Shaft Huts	James Baxtoned 37	Stone Mason	Halifax, Yks	19	15
Shaft Huts	Alfred Bowers 45	Rly Miner	Wiltshire	9	8
Shaft Huts	John Pilkington 40	Rly Miner	Haslingden, Lancs	10	6
Shaft Huts	Isaac Gardiner 32	Rly Miner	Disley, Glos	12	10
Low Smithy	John Jackson 40	Stone Mason	Cark, Lancs	6	1
Bladeses	William Daniels 28	Rly Carter	Wiltshire	6	3
Lowraw	Samuel Bright 29	Stone Mason	Bishop's Castle	8	2
Pinfold	Joseph Carter 29	Rly Labourer	Oxfordshire	10	5
Paradise	George Williams	Rly Miner	Gloucester	7	2

2: Settle-Carlisle Navvies in 1871: Mallerstang

Looking at the enumerator's records of the 1871 Census, there were two types of accommodation in which the navvies and their families lived, writes Peter Robinson.

The popular image is of the hutted encampments that were built by the contractors to house their workers convenient to the major works such as tunnels and viaducts. On Census night in 1871 (April 2) a total number of 225 persons were recorded in two camps in Mallerstang. These were at Aisgill, where 9 huts housed a total of 91 individuals, and at Birkett, where there were 13 huts with 131 inhabitants.

Of this total of 322 there were 85 unskilled workers (labourers, excavators and miners) at Birkett and 9 skilled or supervisory workers (masons, carpenters, foremen, supervisors, etc) while at Aisgill the equivalent numbers were 52 and 8, plus civil engineer George Parry, who lived at Hut 13 with his family. Hut 5 was occupied by James Wilson, grocer, recorded as married but having no wife or family present on Census night. He provided lodgings for John Robinson, his wife and two young daughters.

Away from the camps, numbers of railway workers lived with the local community, either lodging with local families or renting accommodation. The distinction is not always clear, but in Mallerstang the enumerator was better than many in making the necessary distinction. There were, of course, also members of local families who worked for the railway, especially young men, who would eagerly take this opportunity of earning high wages while available on their doorstep. It would be interesting to know how many of these were tempted to follow their employers to contracting work elsewhere.

Within the parish, though not in the camps, were a total of 64 such workers, including 10 in the supervisory or skilled categories, and an Assistant Engineer, Richard Waller, who rented accommodation for his wife and daughter at Hellgill.

Location of railway workers and households in 1871 –

Address	Householder/Age	Occupation	Born	Number in H/H	Rly Wkrs
Southwaite	William Parker 36	Foreman	Glos	19	11
Southwaite	Richard Atkinson 29	Rly Labourer	Windermere	12	8
Castlethwaite	James Ellwood 49	Farmer 40 acres	Mallerstang		1
Castlethwaite	Robert Hutchinson 58	Schoolmaster	Mallerstang		1
Tollbar	Richard Wilson 24	Toll Collector	Yks	8	3
Outhgate	Christopher Watkin 34	Rly Labourer	Richmond, Yks	12	6
Outhgate	Joseph Park 38	Rly Labourer	Sedbergh	5	1
Sycamore Trees	David Shipley 50	Rly Labourer	Yks	18	11
Shorgill	Thomas Murray 27	Rly Labourer	Crosby Rav	2	1
Shorgill	Chris Brunskill 63	Rly Labourer	Kby Stephen	4	2
Shorgill	William Helme 35	Blacksmith	Sandside, Westm	9	6
High Cocklake	Mark Ellwood, 60	Rly Labourer	Bedford	4	3
Castle Cottage	Alexander Forbes 30	Stone Mason	Scotland	5	1
Castle Cottage	Henry Turner 46	Stone Mason	Yks	6	2
Castle Cottage	Isaac Dowson 35	Stone Mason	Yks	4	2
Birket Huts 1	Frederick Pucknell 31	Rly Labourer	Kent	13	12
Birket Huts 2	Eleanor Walker 41	Hut Keeper	Cockermouth	8	4
Birket Huts 3	James Clifford 37	Rly Labourer	Wilts	14	8
Birket Huts 4	John Lewis 58	Rly Labourer	Shrops	10	8
Birket Huts 5	Ann Lyson 41	Hut Keeper	Scotland	15	11
Birket Huts 6	William Emery 48	Miner	Northants	10	8
Birket Huts 7	John Fountain 27	Rly Labourer	Ely, Cambs	5	4
Birket Huts 8	James Jones 42	Horsekeeper	Worcester	12	11
Birket Huts 9	Thomas Wild 55	Rly Labourer	Cheshire	7	6
Birket Huts 10	George Hope 39	Blacksmith	Askham, Westm	11	6
Birket Huts 11	George Scott 31	Foreman Exc	Dumfries	15	12
Birket Huts 12	Thomas Briggs 49	Foreman Exc	Milnthorpe, Westm	9	5
Birket Huts 13	Philip Ayres 27	Superintendent	Kent	6	1
High House	Samuel Evans 62	Rly Labourer	Dorset	10	4
Ais Gill Hut 1	Anthony Troughton 38	Timekeeper	Cumberland	5	2
Ais Gill Hut 2	William Johnson 45	Rly Labourer	Scotland	12	10
Ais Gill Hut 3	in building?				
Ais Gill Hut 4	James Dewer 46	Rly Labourer	Aberdeen	7	6
Ais Gill Hut 5	James Wilson 26	Grocer	Orton, Westm	5	1
Ais Gill Hut 6	Richard Briggs 58	Labourer	Somerset	14	11
Ais Gill Hut 7	William Wallace 64	Labourer	Cumberland	14	9
Ais Gill Hut 8	John Bain 63	Housekeeper	Milnthorpe	18	13
Ais Gill Hut 9	George Parry 51	Civil Engineer	Worcestershire	4	2
Moor Riggs	James Chisholme 25	Rly Labourer	Scotland	5	1
Helgill	Richard Waller 26	Asst to Engineer	Yks	3	1
(not stated)	Joseph Turner 45	Rly Labourer	Cumberland	1	1

3: New Memorial in St Mary's Church, Mallerstang

At a service on May, 2, 1998, the men, women and children of Birkett Huts, Aisgill Huts, Incline Huts and Far Ground who died during the construction of the railway and are buried in St Mary's Churchyard were commemorated by the unveiling of a memorial.

The commemoration was in two parts – indoors, then outdoors. The Rev Iain F MacDougall, senior curate at Kirkby Stephen, conducted a short service inside St Mary's. Canon Bill Greetham, who for many years was vicar of Kirkby Stephen, with spiritual oversight of Mallerstang, intoned names and ages from a list of 25 people who died in "railway time."

The unveiling of a commemorative stone took place in a corner of the churchyard, beside a timeless yew tree. Norman Guy, a former signalman on the Settle-Carlisle, performed the ceremony. The Kirkby Stephen Band accompanied the singing of Abide with Me.

Those who are commemorated:

Name	Date of Burial	Age
Sarah Walker	21.7.1870	3 days
Mary Ridley	8.12.1870	Baby
William Ridley	20.12.1870	Father of above
John Whittal	7.6.1871	32
John Bradbury	1.8.1871	33
John Shaw	21.8.1871	30
James Stephenson	30.5.1872	Twin babies
Richard Stephenson	20.7.1872	ditto
Hannah Staphenson	20.7.1872	34. Mother of above
Edmund F Driver	6.9.1872	3 weeks
Thomas Wyles	8.1.1873	60
William Morris	21.11.1873	26
Miriam Taylor	12.12.1873	4 months
Louisa Garlick	13.12.1874	2 years 6 months
Alice Martin	4.3.1874	10 months

John Stephenson	7.3.1874	47
George Stewart	28.3.1874	36
Thomas Hayley	15.5.1874	32
Caleb Wright	25.5.1874	23
Henry Clifford	23.10.1874	2
James Woodcock	24.10.1874	16
Ellen Chisholme	6.12.1874	4 years 6 months
Sarah Real	10.3.1875	1
James Bel	2.4.1875	38
John Green	8.5.1875	45

4: From the Land Plan of the Midland Railway Company (1912)

The Midland Plan gives a good idea of the ponderous embankments on either side of Moorcock Viaduct, also known as Dandry Mire. Originally, an embankment was proposed but the soft ground accepted all the spoil that was offered with little visible effect except a bulging of the ground at the extremities. A viaduct of 12-spans, a length of 227 yards and maximum height of 50ft was begun at a late stage of railway construction. Note the single track heading from Garsdale to Hawes.

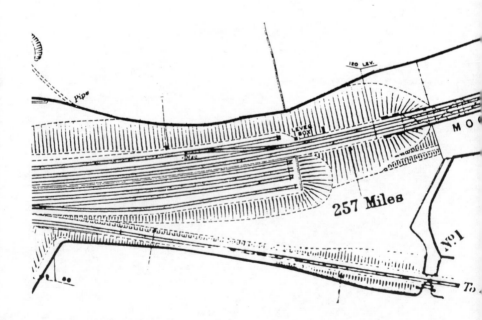

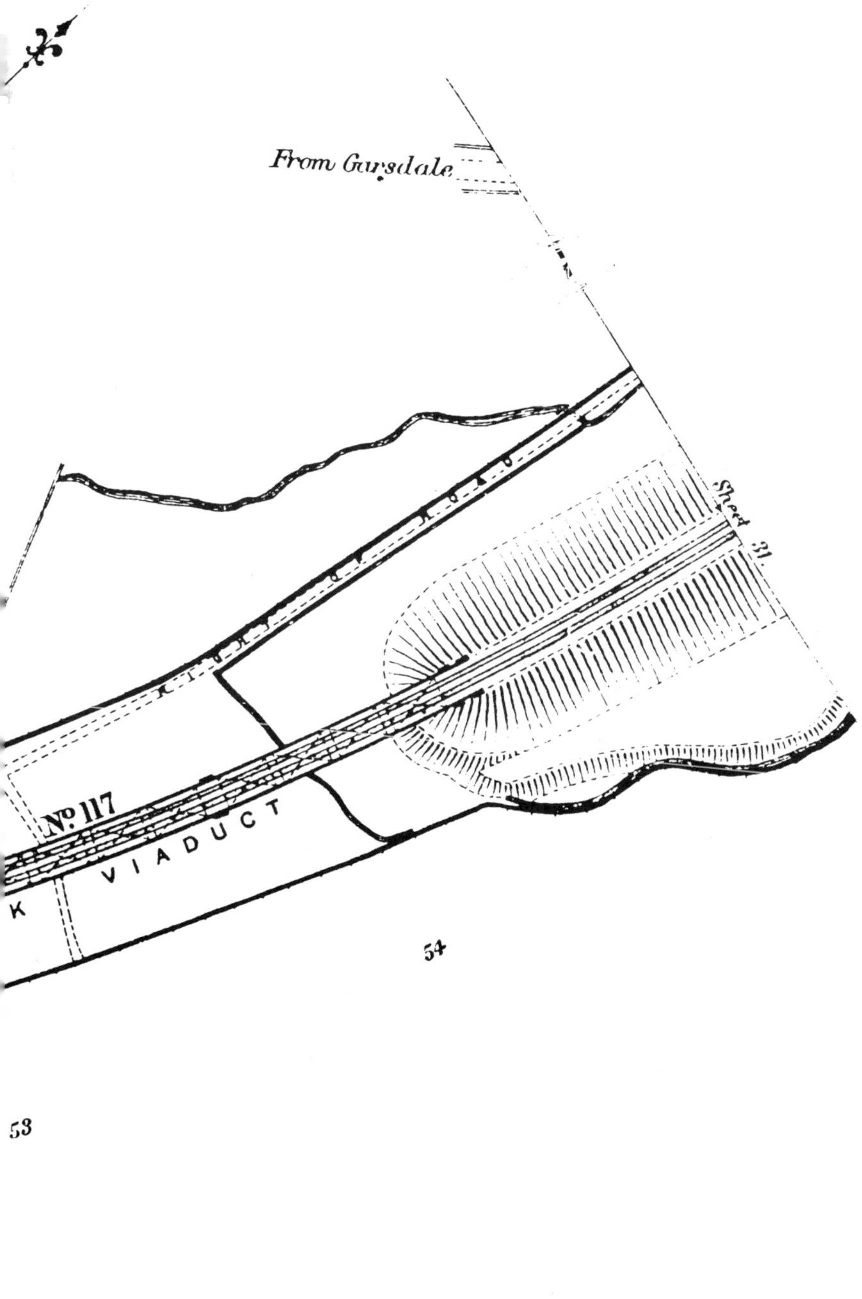

From Garsdale

Sheet 51.

No 117

K VIADUCT

54

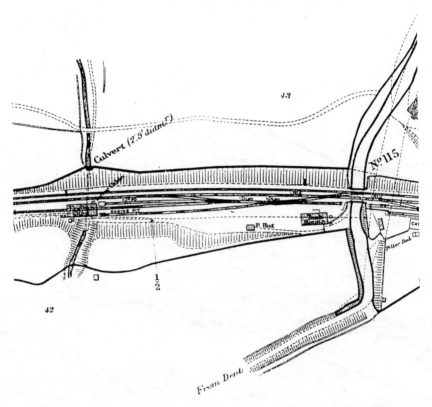

Facilities to the south of Garsdale station, as shown on this Midland company plan, include the engine shed, an engine pit and the Tank House, which was subsequently used as a social centre, with a redundant Midland carriage attached to it as a refreshment room. The Tank House was demolished in 1971.

Acknowledgements

The support of The Settle-Carlisle Railway Development Company is warmly acknowledged. Facts, figures and anecdotes were forthcoming from Pat Brown, Peter Fox, Ron Greenwood, Ralph and Barbara Lake, Margaret Metcalfe, Bell Pratt and Arthur Rudd. Peter Fox not only provided most of the illustrations but gave much-appreciated advice about their display. Paul A Kampen's research based on the Census returns for "railway time" give added historical "body." Peter Robinson kindly provided the appendices relating to the census of 1871 in Garsdale and Mallerstang. Data for the intervening part of the North Riding between the Moorcock and Aisgill awaits collection from the Record Office.

Photographs

W R Mitchell: cover pictures, 39 (bottom), 91, 95
Ralph Lake Collection: 33, 34, 35, 37, 38
Peter Fox: 40 (bottom), 89, 90, 92-93, 96
Paul Holden: 94
John Bull: 36
Margaret Metcalfe Collection: 40 (top).

Aisgill in the days of the Midland Company.